Puffin Books

WORD BOX

Words, words, words! Where do they come from? Who invented them? What are they? Look no further than WORD BOX for an original, exciting companion to speech, the way we talk, what we mean and what our friends think we mean.

English is the richest language in the world. The *Oxford English Dictionary* lists half a million words! In comparison, the German language consists of around 185,000 words, while the French has a mere 100,000. The English we use today is made up of words which came originally from the Celts, the Anglo-Saxons, the Greeks, the Romans, the French and the Germans, to name but a few. There are also words from America, Canada, Australia, Africa, India – and all that is before we start talking about local dialects and that very common form of speech, slang! You might think you know what you're talking about, but armed with this book you are sure to have the last word.

Gyles Brandreth is the author of many books of quizzes, puzzles and jokes. He is also a well-known children's television personality. He lives in London with his wife and three children.

Gyles Brandreth

WORD BOX

Illustrated by Tony Blundell

Puffin Books

PUFFIN BOOKS

Published by the Penguin Group
27 Wrights Lane, London w8 5tz, England
Viking Penguin Inc., 40 West 23rd Street, New York, New York 10010, USA
Penguin Books Australia Ltd, Ringwood, Victoria, Australia
Penguin Books Canada Ltd, 2801 John Street, Markham, Ontario, Canada l3r 1b4
Penguin Books (NZ) Ltd, 182–190 Wairau Road, Auckland 10, New Zealand

Penguin Books Ltd, Registered Offices: Harmondsworth, Middlesex, England

First published 1988

Made and printed in Great Britain by
Richard Clay Ltd, Bungay, Suffolk
Filmset in 11½ on 13 pt Monophoto Palatino

Contents

A Alphabet Soup

Words, words, words! Where do they come from? Who invented them? What are they?

In a nutshell, words are the material we use for communication. Most animals communicate with each other, and sometimes with us, by means of grunts and growls, squeals and barks. If you have a pet you will probably know that it has a range of sounds with which it can communicate different messages. The 'I'm pleased to see you' sounds are different from the 'It's dinner time' ones

and the 'I want to play' ones. Human language probably evolved from a series of grunts and growls, too.

The earliest known writing dates from about 4,000 years BC, but humans were communicating in speech long before that. From early beginnings, thousands of languages have evolved over thousands of years. In *Word box* we are concerned with just one of those languages, English.

English is the richest language in the world. The *Oxford English Dictionary* lists half a million words, and there are probably another half-million technical terms in existence, too. In comparison, the German language consists of 185,000, while the French has a mere 100,000.

English is spoken by about 320 million people, and this is one reason why it is so rich. It has derived from many different sources. In English today we use words that came originally from the Celts, the Anglo-Saxons, the Greeks, the Romans, the French and the Germans, to name just a few. When the British colonized America, Canada, Africa, Australia, India and the Far East, they returned home with further words to add to the English language.

Individual writers have contributed words to our language. William Shakespeare alone came up with some 1,700 of them: words like **suspicious**, **bump**, **hurry** and **lonely**. The Earl of Sandwich, the Duke of Wellington, Louis Braille and Charles Macintosh gave their names to objects that have become household words. World events throw up their own words: the First World War produced words like **cushy** and **camouflage**; the Second, **blitz**, **blackout** and **jeep**.

Nowadays many new words are produced by technology, and by the worlds of advertising, television and newspapers. The computer world has produced terms like **floppy disc**. Television has introduced us to the **video**. The advertising campaign for milk has given the word **bottle** a new meaning: as well as being a glass container, it now means strength and vitality, too.

Some people do not like the introduction of new words, fearing that the language is being debased and turned into slang. This fear is not new. In the eighteenth century Jonathan Swift thought that words like **banter** and **mob** should be done away with; and Dr Johnson disapproved of **clever** and **stingy**.

Language is a living thing that develops all the time. Current English includes all of the following: 'standard English' — that which is considered correct and should be capable of being understood by anyone; colloquial English — that which is spoken and informal; dialect words — particular to that part of the country where they originated, and sometimes not understood by people from elsewhere; slang — similar to colloquial English but even less conventional, and sometimes particular to a certain section of the community; and many technical words which are specific to trades and professions and not widely understood outside them.

In *Word Box* you will find an A to Z of words of all kinds: old words, odd words, silly words, slang words, American words, Australian words, words that will puzzle you, words that will please you and words that will amuse and amaze you. If you come across a word in the book that you don't understand, look it up in a dictionary to see what it means. And if, when you have finished the book, you would like to add a word of your own to the language, do let me know. There's always room for good new words; so if you think you've thought of one that's original and all yours, drop me a line and tell me what it is and what it means. Then, as they say, I'll do my best to help spread the word.

This is the address:

Gyles Brandreth
Word Box
Puffin Books
27 Wrights Lane
London, W8 5TZ

B Blindworms Aren't Blind

Not only is a **blindworm** not blind, it isn't even a worm.
It is a small legless lizard with tiny eyes. It is possible that
people once believed it was a worm (because it had no
legs) and that it had no eyes (because they were so small
they could not easily be seen). The case of the blindworm
heads this chapter because it is a good illustration of how
certain words are not at all what they appear to be at first
sight.

Let's look at some more examples from the animal
kingdom. A **guinea-pig** isn't a pig and it doesn't come
from Guinea. And a **water-rat** isn't a rat; it's a vole,
though it does spend a lot of its time in water. Similarly, a
titmouse is not a mouse, but a small bird. And the **nut-
hatch** may sound like a squirrel-larder, but it's really a
bird as well.

When we get to sea creatures, we are in even deeper
water because a **sea-mouse** is actually a worm, a **sea-fox**

is in fact a shark, a **sea-hog** is a porpoise, and a **sea leopard** is a seal. (By the way, talking of leopards, our ancestors invented a wonderful word for the animal they believed to be a cross between a camel and a leopard. They called it a **camelopard**. We call it a giraffe. Of course the British are not alone in calling animals by strange and seemingly unrelated names. For example, Italians call woodlice *porcellini di Sant' Antonio*, meaning 'piglets of St Anthony'!)

The English language is full of interesting words that turn out not to mean what they look and sound as if they ought to mean. **Doggerel** has nothing to do with dogs, but means rather bad poetry; a **diva** is not a swimming ace but a singer; and **friable** means easily crumbled, not 'able to be fried'. It can be very confusing. For example, **intermine** means 'to penetrate with mines', but **interminable** means never-ending.

There are many pairs of words that sound much the same, but are spelt slightly differently and have very different meanings. **Forbear** means to abstain and is a verb, but **forebear** means an ancestor and is a noun. **Indict** means to accuse by legal process, but **indite** means to put into words. A **bogie** is a kind of railway truck, but a **bogy** is a ghost and a **bogey** is a good score in golf. See if you know the meanings of the words in the following list: They may not all be what they appear to be ...

1. **biannual**
2. **biennial**
3. **canasta**
4. **canister**
5. **comforter**
6. **comforter**
7. **dinghy**
8. **dingy**
9. **noisome**
10. **noisy**

(Answers on page 155.)

C Coffee Pots and Donkeys

What has a coffee pot to do with a donkey? Not a lot, except that they are both the names of word games, and you don't need a pencil or a piece of paper to play them, because they are spoken games. I have put them at the beginning and end of this chapter, with four other firm favourites in between.

Coffee Pot

In this game one player goes out of the room while the others choose a word, which must be a verb, or 'doing'

word. When the word has been decided upon, the player returns, and asks the others ten questions, substituting the words **coffee pot** for the secret verb. For example, he or she might ask, 'Can I coffee pot in the garden?' 'Could I coffee pot if I were at school?' The other players must answer sensibly and honestly, and at the end of the ten questions the questioner has to try and guess the verb. If he or she guesses correctly, a point is scored and someone else has a go at guessing. The first player to score five points wins.

I Packed My Bag

In order to succeed in this game you need an excellent memory, for you have to keep track of an ever-lengthening list of things. The greater the number of players, the more difficult it is. The first player starts by saying, 'I packed my bag and in it I put' — here they can choose anything they like — 'my hair brush.' The second player says, 'I packed by bag and in it I put my hair brush and my toothbrush.' The third player says, 'I packed my bag and in it I put my hair brush, my toothbrush and a bar of chocolate.' The fourth player says, 'I packed my bag and in it I put my hair brush, my toothbrush, a bar of chocolate and my pyjamas,' and so it continues, round and round the group of players, with each one repeating the previous list and adding an item of his or her own. If someone forgets an item in the list, or recites them in the wrong order, then he or she drops out. The player who stays in the longest wins.

The Moulting Ostrich

This game is as funny as its title. The players stand round in a circle, with one member in the centre. His or her job is to make the others laugh, and *their* job is to resist any attempt even to make them smile. It works like this.

The player in the centre addresses each member of the circle in turn, saying, 'Alas, my poor ostrich is moulting and I don't know what to do.' The person addressed then has to make a suggestion, without laughing him- or herself and without making any other member of the circle laugh. The player in the centre can laugh as much as he or she likes. Any players in the circle who can't keep a straight face drop out.

Players' suggestions might be something like these:

'Buy it some hair oil.'

'Feed it on spinach.'

'Ost-racize it.'

If some or all of the players survive the first round without laughing, the one in the centre goes round again. This time he says, 'Alas, alas, my poor ostrich is moulting and I've got a boil on the end of my nose and I don't know what to do.'

This time the players might reply:

'Stick ostrich feathers on your nose.'

'Feed your nose on spinach.'

'Glue the feathers on the ostrich and stick a plaster on your nose. Or do it the other way around.'

Those players who survive into the third round are faced with, 'Alas, alas, alas, my poor ostrich is moulting, I've got a boil on the end of my nose and my turkey's lost its stuffing and I don't know what to do.'

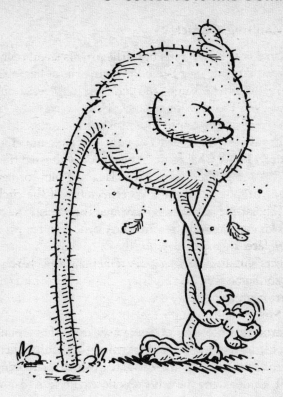

Anyone who manages to get through all three rounds without giggling or smiling wins, and takes a turn in the centre.

The Minister's Cat

This word game tests your vocabulary, that is to say the number of words you know. It is an alphabetical game that can be played with any number of people.

The first player starts by saying: 'The minister's cat is an adorable cat and its name is Adam,' in other words, giving first a word to describe the cat and then a name for the cat, both beginning with A. The second player has B, and so might say, 'The minister's cat is a black cat and its name is Barney.' So play continues, going round and round the players and through the alphabet successfully. (You might decide beforehand to omit awkward letters like X and Z.) Anyone who cannot come up with both an adjective to describe the cat and a name for it loses a point, as does anyone who repeats anything said previously, for if you are good at this game you may go through the alphabet more than once. The player who has lost the least number of points when you all agree to stop is the winner.

I Want a Rhyme

This is a game for four or more players. One is chosen as leader, and calls out: 'I want a rhyme in jolly quick time, and the word I choose is *pen*.' (The word chosen must be one that will rhyme with a number of others.) Each player in turn then has to say a word that rhymes with pen, such as den, ten, hen, men, and so on. Anyone who can't think of a rhyming word drops out, until the last person left in wins that round and takes his or her turn to be leader and call out a new word.

Donkey

Donkey is a word-building game for two or more players. Each player in turn calls out a letter, with a view to building a word of four or more letters. The aim of the game is not to finish a word yourself but to force one of your opponents to do just that. For example, if Tom and Jerry were playing, the game might go like this:

TOM: C (He is thinking of 'cook'.)

JERRY: C-A (He is thinking of 'cartoon'.)

TOM: C-A-R (He knows that three-letter words don't count and he is now thinking of 'carnival'.)

JERRY: C-A-R-T (Poor Jerry, he's out! He was thinking of 'cartoon', which would have ended with Tom, but he forgot that 'cart' is also a word, and he's completed it, so that's that.)

Each time a player finishes a word, he or she loses a life. Players have six lives each; the first player to have lost all six is the DONKEY and loses the game.

You can also lose a life if you offer a letter that doesn't belong in a real word and the next player challenges you. For example, if Tom had said, 'C-A-R-J,' Jerry could have challenged him, and Tom would have lost a life because there isn't a word that begins 'carj'. But if Tom had said

'C-A-R-G,' and Jerry had challenged him, Jerry would have lost a life — because there *is* a word that begins 'carg'. Can you think of it? (Answer on page 155.)

D   Dingoes, Didgeridoos and Dilly-bags

If this chapter's heading were to be printed upside down, it would confirm what you already suspect — that this chapter is all about Australian words. Australia is a vast country of 7,690,000 square kilometres (2,970,000 square miles) and a population of 12,728,000. Apart from its Aboriginal inhabitants, who now number about 70,000, all of the population of Australia has arrived since Captain Cook landed there in 1770, and they come from many

different regions of the world. For this reason Australian English is a mixture of Aboriginal words, dialect English, imported words, slang, and robust, no-nonsense words coined by the outback farmers who lived a rough, tough life.

Let's look first at some Aboriginal words. A **dingo** is a half-wild Australian dog, and the name has also come to mean a treacherous person. To **dingo on** is to betray. A **didgeridoo** is a very long, horn-like instrument whose

sound is like its name, which is how it came to be so called. If you know the words of 'Waltzing Matilda', you will have come across a **jumbuck**, which came to drink at a **billabong**. These are both Aboriginal words; a jumbuck is a sheep, a billabong is a pool, from the Aboriginal word *billa*, meaning water. This has also given us another word which is known throughout the world: **billycan** or **billy**, a cross between a kettle and a teapot which is filled with water and put on the fire to boil and brew the tea. And to rhyme with billy we have a **dilly-bag**, a haversack, wallet or shopping bag, which comes from the word *dilli*, meaning a basket.

Some words which are nowadays thought of as being typically Australian were originally dialect or colloquial expressions from various parts of England, showing where some Australians come from. **Wowser**, for example, meaning 'a killjoy', comes from the north of England; **cobber**, 'a friend', from Suffolk; **corker**, 'a good thing', from Ireland; and **dinkum**, 'genuine, honest or thorough', from Lincolnshire.

Australia also has its own rhyming slang, like Cockney. A **Joe Blake** is a snake; **Pat Malone** means alone; **Oscar**, from Oscar Asche, an actor, means cash. A **butcher's**, which in Cockney rhyming slang means a look, in Australian English means angry.

From the gold-mining communities we get **tucker**, meaning rations, and **mullock**, which now means refuse or rubbish, but formerly meant a rock which contained no gold. This word was originally an English dialect word. And from the vast sheep-farms, and itinerant workers, Australian English has collected a number of evocative words and phrases which are nothing if not forthright. A

17

dogger is a dingo hunter; a **bluey** refers to a bushman's bundle, so called from its being commonly wrapped in a blue blanket; a **ratbag** is an unpleasant person; **rough as bags** means uncouth; **cow-cocky** is a dairy farmer; a **drongo** is a lazy or undesirable person; **home on the pig's back** means very successful; to **dip one's lid** means to raise one's hat; to **do a perisher** is to die from lack of water; to be **a bit of a lyre-bird** means to tell lies; **the straight wire** is the genuine thing, especially when applied to authentic news; **bulls' wool** is nonsense; a **Jacky Howe** is a sleeveless shirt, as worn by sheep-shearer John Howe; and, of course, to **waltz Matilda** means to carry one's swag (or bluey).

A number of words commonly used in Britain today were originally Australian slang, for example **cuppa**, meaning a cup of tea, and **tatty**, meaning inferior or cheap. The phrases **too right!**, meaning 'certainly!', came from Australia, as did **the daddy of them all**, meaning the biggest or most notable.

And what of the famous word **pommy**, which we all know means a newcomer, and especially one from England? Well, its origin is disputed, but one theory is that it is short for pomegranate, and that the English were so called because of their ruddy cheeks which easily got burnt in the hot Australian sunshine.

E Eggs Mark the Spot

'Mum, I've had an accident in the kitchen.'

'I know, eggs mark the spot!'

That's a pun, a clever play on words in which a word or words that look or sound the same or very similar are used to raise a smile or a laugh, a groan or a great guffaw. In the case above, the pun was on the word **eggs** which sounds like the letter X.

PATIENT: Doctor, I've got a terrible problem. Sometimes I think I'm a wigwam and sometimes I think I'm a tepee. What's wrong with me?

DOCTOR: You're too tense.

Here the pun is on the phrase **too tense** because, of course, it sounds like 'two tents'.

IRATE DINER: Waiter! This coffee tastes like mud!
WAITER: I'm sorry, sir. It was only ground this morning.

Here the pun is on the word **ground**, which can mean either the ground we walk on, or the past participle of the verb 'to grind'.

Creating pun-filled sentences is great fun. Here are some of my favourites:

'I'm dying,' he croaked.
'My experiment is bubbling nicely,' the chemist retorted.
'The fire's going out,' he bellowed.
'I ordered strawberry, not vanilla,' I screamed.
'Someone's at the door,' she chimed.
'Visitors are coming,' he guessed.
'It was a big black bird,' he crowed.

'Zero,' he answered, naughtily.
'Pass the cards round,' she said, ideally.

Did you spot all the puns? They're awful, aren't they? That's the odd thing about puns; the worse they are, the better they are — if you see what I mean.

You can make riddles out of puns. These are three of my favourites.

When is longhand quicker than shorthand?
When it's on a clock.

What sits and shivers at the bottom of the sea?
A nervous wreck.

What does the Queen do when she burps?
She issues a royal pardon.

Get the idea? Now see if you can solve these riddles. The answer to each one involves a clever play on words.

1. Why is a joke like a coconut?
2. When does a wooden floor feel cold?
3. Why are playing cards like wolves?

4. Why is a crossword puzzle like a quarrel?
5. Why did the man repair the horn of his car?
6. What happens when a flea loses its temper?
7. When can a farmer look at his pigs?
8. Why did the local ants bow to the foreign ant?
9. What is round and bad-tempered?
10. On which day of the year are we commanded to go forward?

(Answers on page 155.)

Try constructing some puns and riddles for yourself. Here is a list of words that could help.

and/'and	none/nun
board/bored	ooze/who's, whose
caught/court	pick (implement, to choose)
drive (to drive, a road)	quay/key
eve/'eave	rain/reign
find/fined	train (transport, to teach)
girl/gull	udder/utter
ham (meat, bad actor)	staid/stayed
in/inn	vowel/foul/fowl
jest/just	wan/one
knead/need	you/ewe/u
loan/lone	zip (a fastener, to dash
Mary/merry	around)

F Floccinaucinihilipilification and Friends

Floccinaucinihilipilification is the longest word in the *Oxford English Dictionary*. It contains twenty-nine letters and it means 'the act or habit of estimating as worthless'. I've included it in the heading because this chapter is all about extraordinary words, like 'floksi' and her friends.

The English language doesn't really go in for long words, unlike German and Swedish (the longest German word is eighty letters long; the longest Swedish word ninety-four letters long), but *Webster's Third International Dictionary* lists a forty-seven-letter word: **pneumono-ultramicroscopicsilicovolcanoconiosises**; it is the plural form of a word meaning a lung disease contracted by miners. **Antidisestablishmentarianism** is 'a movement against the removing of state recognition of an established church' and runs to just twenty-eight letters. **Supercali-**

fragilisticexpialidocious is six letters longer, but it doesn't mean anything; it's a nonsense word made up for the 1964 film *Mary Poppins*.

Of course, a word does not have to be long to make it extraordinary. One of my favourite words is **axolotl**, which budding zoologists will know is a kind of Mexican newt. And is **rhythms** the only English word that contains no vowels? Far from it. There's **cwm**, a Welsh word, pronounced 'coomb'; it can mean a valley, or it can mean a hollow on a mountainside formed in the Ice Age. Another vowel-less word is *styryl*, a kind of chemical.

A lot of strange words are of foreign origin. A **bdellium** is a kind of tree; a **zloty** is a Polish monetary unit; a **zebec** is a Mediterranean sailing ship; a **ylang-ylang** is a Malaysian tree; and a **zho** is a cross between a yak and cow.

Returning to good old English words, what do you suppose a **tom-noddy** is? He is a foolish person. And a **pettichaps**? It sounds a bit like a fellow in a petticoat, but in fact it is a kind of bird. And a **whillywham**? This is a rather unpleasant individual who tries to insinuate himself into your confidence, to flatter and deceive you. A **huff-snuff**, however, is a conceited sort of chap, quick to take offence. To **pudder** is to poke about with your hand or a stick (you could pudder in a pond); to **sneap** is to nip or pinch; to **pind** is to shut in or enclose; to **huggle** someone is to give them a hug; and a **gyle** means the amount brewed in one fermentation. To **dwine** means to waste away. If you are American you might wear a **wamus**, for it is a kind of cardigan in the southern USA.

A **fipple** is the plug at the mouth of a wind instrument that controls its volume; and a **futtock** is one of the middle timbers of a ship. **Inkle** is an old kind of linen tape; **vogt** means a steward or bailiff; **pir** is a Muhammadan saint; a **cryal** is a kind of heron. An **ixia** is a South African flower; a **cuffin** is a slang name for a cove; a **ranny** is a field mouse; **waly** is an old exclamation of sorrow; and **gutta-percha** is the gum of a Malaysian tree. One of my favourites is the **turritellid**, a very humble creature, despite its wonderful name. It's simply a type of snail.

G Good Grief!

Good grief! is an exclamation of surprise. It's a euphemism, too, a polite or roundabout way of expressing something which might otherwise sound offensive, in this case, saying **Good God!** Both **Good grief** and **Good God** are slang expressions. Slang is that part of the language that we all use when we are talking informally; slang, however, doesn't always meet with universal approval.

Almost every walk of life has its own brand of slang. Much of the slang used when I was young derived from expressions first used in the Army, Navy and Air Force, and a lot of it persists today. **Gen**, meaning information, is RAF slang, and comes from orders which read 'For the general information of all concerned . . .' To **fox**, meaning to puzzle, also comes from the armed services, as does that wonderful name for a Cornish pasty, **tiddy oggy**.

Off the beam, meaning 'failing to understand', comes from a 1938 RAF expression that refers to the wireless beam that guided aircraft in to land in times of bad visibility. Interestingly, the word **boche**, used by British soldiers to mean German soldiers, was originally French slang.

Slang used by people in various trades and professions is similar to jargon. The drapery trade has an expressive phrase meaning absolutely honest: **all wool and a yard wide**. Sailors engaged in cleaning duties on ships would **part brass rags** if they had an argument since, in days gone by, brass-cleaning rags used to be shared. We do a **double take** if we can't quite believe our eyes and have to look at something twice; but this originally meant exactly what it says, and was a term used in the film business when a scene had to be shot twice.

Many of our slang expressions come from the United States. Phrases like **ants in your pants**, meaning 'restless', were originally coined in the States, and came to Britain in

the late 1930s and early 1940s. To **beef**, meaning 'to complain', is American, as is **corny**, meaning 'dull and obvious'. (It is believed to be a reference to the rather unsophisticated and old-fashioned ways of those who live in the Corn Belt region of the USA.) **Cute**, which is another American import, comes from the standard English word *acute* and, somewhere along the line, lost its initial *a*. To **get someone's goat**, meaning 'to annoy', came into being in the States in approximately 1916. To **talk through one's hat**, meaning 'to talk nonsense': to **hit the hay**, meaning 'to go to bed' (a reference to tramps in barns); and to **hock**, meaning 'to pawn', are all American slang. **Hooch**, meaning 'alcohol', is also, but this word comes from a native Alaskan term, *hoochino*, meaning a strong drink. The nicely descriptive **rubber-necking** is a good American term coined in the early years of this

century. It means excessively curious behaviour, and is similar in its imagery to **gander**, meaning to have a good old peer over someone's shoulder. Both imply long supple necks. **Roadhog**, a bad and aggressive driver, is an American phrase, and another farmyard animal, the turkey, lends its name to **talking turkey**, meaning to talk plainly or seriously.

Other countries, too, have lent English their slang words. **Blarney**, the gift of the gab, comes from the custom of kissing the Blarney Stone at Castle Blarney in Ireland. **Chokey**, meaning 'a prison', comes from the Hindustani word *chauki*, a four-sided place or building. Another Hindustani word, *khush*, gives us **cushy** – meaning easy, or safe. To **doss**, to lie down on a makeshift bed,

comes from the Latin word for back, *dorsum*; to **take a dekko** is from the Romany word *dik*, to look or see; **guy is believed to come from the Yiddish word** *goy*, meaning 'Gentile'; **gumption**, common sense or shrewdness, comes from the Scottish word *gawm*; **smithereens**, meaning small fragments, is Anglo-Irish.

Some slang expressions are a good deal older than you might imagine. For example, the word **bumf**, meaning paper, comes from the term **bum-fodder**, which means lavatory paper, and has been in existence since the mid-seventeenth century. **Neddy**, as a name for a donkey, dates back to roughly the same time, while the word **jakes**, meaning a loo, was a standard English word from about 1530 until 1750, after which it was regarded as a colloquialism, that is something belonging to spoken and informal language rather than the kind of phrase that would be written down.

Some slang expressions derive from particular characters. A **card**, meaning an odd or eccentric person, was

so called after a novel called *The Card*, written by Arnold Bennett in 1911; **gamp**, a large umbrella, came from the description of the character, Sarah Gamp, in Charles Dickens's *Martin Chuzzlewit*; having **green fingers**, meaning 'good at gardening', was a phrase coined by a Mr Middleton, who was a gardening journalist and broadcaster.

Here are a few more slang expressions whose meanings and origins may amuse you.

cave!   the Latin word for 'Beware!', it was used by public schoolboys.

chestnut   an old, stale story; from the US phrase 'roast chestnuts', i.e. well-cooked ones.

dago a man from one of the Mediterranean countries. In the seventeenth century, Diego (James) was a nickname for a Spaniard.

dukes fists. This comes from rhyming slang: 'Duke of York's' meant 'forks'; from there it came to mean 'fingers', and from there to mean 'fists'.

gippy (as in 'gippy tummy') meant 'Egyptian', and from there came to mean stomach upsets associated with hot climates.

how's tricks? how are things? From card games, in which 'tricks' are taken.

la-di-da meaning 'posh and affected', comes from a music-hall song of 1880, 'He wears a penny flower in his coat, La-di-da!'

limey from 'lime-juicer', American and Canadian slang for an Englishman; from English sailors' habits of drinking lime juice to avoid scurvy.

loco meaning 'insane', in the USA and Canada; from loco weed, a plant containing a drug that drove animals which ate it temporarily crazy.

murphy a potato, so called from the Irish surname Murphy, the Irish being

renowned for growing and eating potatoes.

paddy
a fit of temper; from an earlier phrase, to **get's one Irish up**, which meant 'to get angry'.

posh
smart. The origin of this word is uncertain, but one interesting theory put forward is that it derives from people travelling to India by ship, and stands for **P**ort **O**ut, **S**tarboard **H**ome, these being the sides of the ship sheltered from the heat of the sun's rays.

scarper
to run away; originally from the Italian verb *scappare*, but rhyming slang made it into Scapa Flow ('go'), as if this were its origin.

sitting pretty   to be in a good position; believed to derive from chickens sitting on the nest.

sure!   meaning 'certainly', 'a pleasure'; originated in early eighteenth-century England, whence it travelled to the USA and back again, so we now think of it as being American slang.

tanner   the name for the old sixpence (6d), which derives from obsolete underworld slang from, surprisingly, the Bible: 'He lodgeth with one Simon, a tanner.'

vamoose   American slang for 'to depart or disappear', from the Spanish, *vamos*, let's go.

yob   a lout or stupid person; comes from the word 'boy' spelt backwards.

zizz   a rest; comes from servicemen's slang and is derived from the sound of snoring.

H Hangman

In the bad old days, people used to be hanged for committing certain crimes. In the really bad old days, you could be hanged for stealing a horse. Happily, this chapter is not about crime or punishment but about pencil-and-paper word games, and Hangman is the name of one of the most popular.

Hangman

This is a game for two people, in which one thinks of a word and writes it down as a number of blanks, then the other has to guess the word, letter by letter. For each wrong guess, part of a gibbet is constructed, and the idea is to guess the word before you are hanged. It works like this.

Player A thinks of a word. It is best to have a longish word, so let us suppose he thinks of 'encyclopedia'. He writes it down as twelve dashes, like this:

- - - - - - - - - - - -

If Player B thinks it might contain an 'a', she will say, 'A', and Player A has to write the letter in where it occurs, like this:

- - - - - - - - - - - A

Player B might then guess, 'E', so the word would look like this:

E - - - - - - - E - - A

If she then guesses, 'B', Player A starts to construct the gibbet, like this:

———

Play continues in this way; if Player B thinks she knows the word, she can guess it in its entirety – but if she's wrong, another part of the gibbet is constructed. I use a gibbet and body made up of eleven components, so the guessing player has eleven chances; but you can devise your own as long as you are consistent about the number of components it has.

The Name Game

Each player needs a piece of paper and a pencil, and ideally someone who isn't playing should time you with a watch. Before you start, you decide a number of categories — something like this:

NAMES OF {
animals
birds
rivers
countries
TV programmes
}

Then, starting with the first category chosen, each player has exactly one minute to write down as many names of animals, or whatever has been chosen, as he or she can think of. The player with the greatest number wins the round, and the players move on to the next category. At the end of the game, the player with the greatest total number wins. A variation of this game is to count only those names *that no one else has written down*.

One Hundred Words

This game is a lot more difficult than it sounds. The aim is to write down a hundred words, in sentences that make sense, without repeating a single word (not even 'a' or 'the'!). The person who finishes first, with a hundred words or as near to that number as possible, wins. Here's what happened when I had a go.

I am sitting at my desk trying to write one hundred words without repeating them. Some challenge! Is it impossible? Sarah thought she could win easily, but by

fifty gave up. Sally managed seventy-five, Maureen sixty-two, Alison forty-six. Andrew didn't produce any. He said composing such lengthy essays was much too difficult on a Monday afternoon before tea when hungry. Oscar, our cat, miaowed loudly, jumped over the table and knocked papers all around. What an animal! Felines are like that – contrary, perverse, mischievous, comfort-loving, always in charge, seldom contrite, utterly uncontrollable, bewitchingly beautiful, amusing – absolutely adorable!

I shan't tell you how long it took me!

Word Ladders

You can play this game on your own or with a friend. The idea is to change one word into another, step by step, changing one letter at each move. Each step in the ladder must be a proper word. For example, P I G can be changed to S T Y like this:

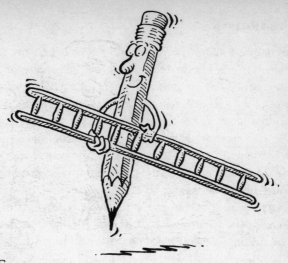

PIG
WIG
WAG
WAY
SAY
STY

Here are some more you could try:

EYE to LID
FLOUR to BREAD
TEA to HOT
MINE to COAL
DOG to CAT

(Answers on page 156.)

Rhyming Consequences

Consequences is a game in which everyone starts with a piece of paper and a pencil; he or she writes down a line or two, before folding the paper and passing it to the next player. No one knows what has gone before; he or she adds another line or two and then folds the paper and passes it on. Sometimes all the players agree to write down the same sort of thing – a person's name or a place-name, for example, or what 'he said' or 'she said'.

In Rhyming Consequences, the first player writes two rhyming lines, folds over the paper, and then adds half of a third line. The next player completes the third line without looking at the previous two, writes two more, then folds the paper and adds half of another line, before passing it on. Play continues until the bottom of the paper has been reached, after which the papers are unfolded and read out. The results are often extremely funny.

For example, the first player may write:

> Susie was a large black pig,
> On Sundays she wore an orange wig,
> Which gave her

The next player would only see 'Which gave her', and might write:

> . . . a black eye from time to time,
> Which didn't really look sublime.
> She cured it when she ate a lime,
> Which tasted

Then the next player might add:

> . . . like school fish and chips.

And so it would continue.

This is a great game, even if it isn't the way to write great poetry!

I I Before E Except After C

Most people will recognize this chapter title as one of the rules of spelling. In English, I always comes before E except after C. Or does it? How many of the words below are spelt correctly?

believe	mien	shield
deceive	neigh	shriek
feign	niece	thief
feint	receive	tier
forfeit	rein	wield
grieve	seismic	
leisure	seize	

How many obey the 'I before E except after C' rule? Eleven out of nineteen do. Are only eleven words spelt correctly? Well, I'm afraid the answer to that question is 'No'. *All* the words listed above are spelt correctly, despite the rule.

This is the problem with English spelling. There are rules, and most words obey them — but not all do.

For example, a number of verbs double their last letter and add 'ing' to form the present participle, and 'er' to form the noun (such as: **travel**, **travelling**, **traveller**; **swim**, **swimming**, **swimmer**; **run**, **running**, **runner**). Verbs ending in 'e' (such as **drive**) drop the 'e' before adding the 'ing' but retain it before the final 'r' (as in **drive**, **driving**, **driver**; **ride**, **riding**, **rider**; **write**, **writing**, **writer**). But what about **type**? Instead of **type**, **typing**, **typer**, it becomes **type**, **typing**, **typist**. And **style** becomes **style**, **styling**, **stylist**.

For me, the most difficult problem with English spelling is in words of several syllables where double consonants occur. Is it **necessary** or **neccesary**? **Spaghetti** or **spaggheti**? **Piccolo** or **picollo**? If you think you can spell, try spotting which of the words below are correct and which are incorrect. And don't forget the three above!

accomodation   flourescence   permissable
coolly   harrassment   posession
definitely   investegate   rythm
disappointment   malicious   seperate
ecstacy   manageable   threshold
excusible   occurence   vocabulary
exuberant   parallel   woolly

(Answers on page 156.)

J Jumbo Was an Elephant

Jumbo really was an elephant. He was an African elephant bought by Regent's Park Zoo in 1865 from the Paris Zoo, and was the first African elephant London had owned. He was very large (even for an elephant!), standing 3.3 metres high (nearly 11 feet) and weighing 6.5 tonnes. Jumbo became very popular, and there was an outcry among the British public when it was decided to sell him to Phineas T. Barnum's circus in America. A number of popular songs were written about him, and even Queen Victoria protested that he should remain in Britain. But it was all to no

avail, for he went to America, to become popular with children there until his untimely end three and a half years later when he was hit by a train and killed. His name became synonymous with the word 'elephant'; over the years 'Jumbo' has been used to describe anything very large. Hence we have jumbo jets, jumbo packets of washing powder, and so on. A word that derives from a name, as **jumbo** was, is called an eponym, and there are lots of them in everyday use. This chapter looks at the origins of some of the better-known ones.

Ampère

If you study physics you will know that an ampère is the unit of measurement for electric current; even if you don't, you will probably have heard of a 15-amp plug or fuse. The unit is named after André Marie Ampère, a French physicist who lived between 1775 and 1836 and who discovered that there is a link between magnetism and electricity.

Biro

The word commonly used for the ballpoint pen was the surname of its inventor. László Biró was a Hungarian who invented the ballpoint pen in 1938. It became very popular during the Second World War because, unlike the fountain pen, it did not leak at high altitudes and so could be used in aircraft. Biró had an English company lined up to manufacture his pens at the end of the war, but it was taken over by a French firm owned by Baron Biche. And his ballpoint pens were called – yes, you've guessed it – *Bics*.

Bloomers

Nowadays, we tend to think of 'bloomers' as being loose, baggy trousers, or as an alternative word for knickers; but in the 1850s the word meant a complete outfit for women, consisting of a top, a skirt ending between the knees and ankles and, underneath it, baggy trousers held in at the ankles. The costume was designed by an American lady, Mrs Amelia Bloomer, who was a nineteenth-century version of what today would be called a feminist, and who thought that the clothes women had to wear in her day were impractical and uncomfortable. Her outfit was ridiculed, but found favour forty years later when women began to ride bicycles. By then the word **bloomers** was applied only to the trousers.

Bobby

This word for a policeman derives from the name of Sir Robert Peel, who, as Home Secretary, formed the first

police force in Britain in 1829. It operated in London, and its members were called 'peelers' or 'bobbies', after Sir Robert. By the middle of the nineteenth century most towns in Britain had their own police force, and the name **bobby** stuck.

Bowdlerize

You may not be familiar with this word, but it means 'to censor'. Dr Thomas Bowdler was an eighteenth-century English physician who was shocked by some of the rather coarse words and expressions used by Shakespeare, so he set himself the task of producing a censored edition of Shakespeare's plays which could be read aloud in front of the family without embarrassment. His work gained a lot

of publicity and, though some people thought his ideas were ridiculous, in the nineteenth century the word **bowdlerize** came to describe censorship for reasons of politeness.

Bowie knife

The Bowie knife was named after Colonel Jim Bowie who fought alongside Davy Crockett at the Battle of the Alamo in 1836. Bowie had invented the knife nine years earlier and credited it with saving his life in a fight. The knife, between 25 and 38 centimetres (10–15 inches) long, and curved at the tip, was much admired and Bowie had copies made with a two-edged blade. They were sold as **Bowie knives**.

Bowler hat

We think of bowler hats as being the badge of the City

gent, but they were originally designed to be worn while riding horses, and indeed are still worn for that purpose. In the nineteenth century, a Norfolk landowner named William Coke became tired of losing his tall hat when riding; he asked a hatter called Mr Beaulieu to design headgear that would fit more snugly on his head. **Bowler** is the English corruption of the French word *Beaulieu*.

Boycott

This word, meaning 'to shun', derives from the name of Charles Cunningham Boycott, an English farmer and land-agent in Ireland's County Mayo in the second half of the nineteenth century. There was a good deal of unrest among Irish tenant-farmers at that time, and they formed a Land League to protect their interests. Those on Lord Erne's estate, for which Boycott was agent, asked for a reduction in their rent. Boycott refused, so the local people tried to force him to change his mind. Shopkeepers refused to serve him, men refused to work on his land, the blacksmith refused to shoe his horses and, in the end, he was forced to leave the district. Thus his name became used to mean ostracism, or shunning, of something or somebody.

Braille

Louis Braille was born in France in 1809; as a small child he suffered an accident which left him blind in both eyes. He was sent to the National Institute for the Blind in Paris, where the only books for the blind were written in large embossed letters, making them very big and cumbersome. Braille heard of an invention by an army captain called Charles Barbier, in which dots were used to punch messages on to pieces of card so that they could be read at night. Braille perfected the system, working out an alphabet, symbols for '**and**', '**for**' and other commonplace words, and even musical notation.

Cardigan

The familiar button-down-the-front woolly was named after the seventh Earl of Cardigan, who lived from 1797 to 1868 and led the charge of the Light Brigade at the Battle of Balaclava in 1854. He wore a knitted woollen waistcoat to keep out the cold; and this garment, with or without sleeves, came to be named after him. The knitted woollen hat called the **balaclava** was named after the battle, too.

Chauvinist

This word, originally meaning someone with an exaggerated sense of national pride, but now extended to include someone who believes in the superiority of men over women, derived from a Frenchman called Nicolas Chauvin. He was so devoted to Napoleon, admiring him absolutely and refusing to hear a word against him, that he became an object of ridicule, and the word **chauvinist** became popular to mean anyone utterly devoted to a country or a cause.

Clerihew

Edmund Clerihew Bentley was a writer who invented a new form of verse when he was sixteen. It had four lines, the first two and last two of which rhymed with each other; but it did not have to scan, and it generally made some kind of satirical statement about someone. Here is Bentley's first effort:

> Sir Humphry Davy
> Abominated gravy.
> He lived in the odium
> Of having discovered sodium.

His rhymes became as popular as limericks and were published in a book by 'E. Clerihew', after which this form of verse became known as a **clerihew**.

Diesel

Rudolf Diesel was a German who studied engineering in the 1870s and set about producing a new kind of engine which was more efficient than its predecessors. It took a long time — and nearly killed him, when one blew up — but in the end he managed to produce a type of internal-combustion engine which ran on a low-grade, partly refined oil. Today the word **diesel** is used for both the engine and the fuel.

Guillotine

You may think of a guillotine as a device for cutting paper, but its name comes from the grisly invention of Dr Joseph Guillotin who designed it as a painless method of execution during the French Revolution. It was first used in 1792.

Hooligan

This familiar term for someone who behaves badly (never let it be said about *you*) is a corruption of the name Houlihan. The Houlihans were a large and boisterous Irish family who lived in Southwark, London, in the nineteenth century, and whose exploits led to much gossip. In time, their name came to be used to mean 'bad and unruly behaviour'.

July

The seventh month of the year, which in the old Roman calendar was the fifth month and called *Quintilis*, was renamed by Julius Caesar after himself. Caesar was born on 12 July 100 BC.

Mach number

In these days of supersonic airliners we have become familiar with expressions like 'Mach 2'; but the name comes from an Austrian physicist called Ernst Mach who was born in Moravia in 1838. A **Mach** compares the speed of a particular flight to the speed of sound at sea level. Mach 1 is 1,207 kilometres per hour (750 mph), the speed of sound.

Mackintosh

Nearly everybody's wardrobe contains a **mackintosh**, but the garment was unheard of until a Glasgow chemist called Charles Macintosh discovered that when naphtha (a substance obtained when tar is distilled) is amalgamated with indiarubber, it will bind two pieces of cloth together and make them waterproof. Macintosh patented his invention in 1823, and the first raincoat was produced in 1830.

Pasteurize

Pasteurization is a process by which milk is heated to a high temperature and then cooled rapidly in order to kill bacteria in it. It was invented by the famous French chemist Louis Pasteur in the 1860s as a way of killing the microbes that were ruining the French wine harvest.

Peach Melba

This delicious dessert made from fresh peaches, cream, ice-cream and raspberry sauce was created by the famous French chef Escoffier in honour of Dame Nellie Melba, the Australian opera singer. In fact Dame Nellie's surname was Mitchell, but she adopted the stage name Melba because of its similarity to the city of her birth, Melbourne. A raspberry sauce is often called a **melba** sauce. Melba toast (very thin, crisp toast) was also created for Dame Nellie.

Plimsolls and the Plimsoll Line

Samuel Plimsoll, Liberal Member of Parliament for Derby, was interested in merchant shipping. He successfully campaigned for a law (passed in 1876) to force every ship to be marked with a line beyond which it could not safely be loaded. This line became known as the **Plimsoll Line**; it helped save many lives and many ships. The rubber-soled shoes that also bear his name are believed to be so called because the original design of the sole resembled the Plimsoll Line on a ship.

Sam Browne

A **Sam Browne**, invented in the 1880s, was originally a leather belt with an extra strap across the right shoulder, worn as a sword-belt by soldiers in the British Army and named after its inventor, General Sir Samuel Browne. A light-reflecting version of the Sam Browne is often worn by cyclists and motor-cyclists in the dark nowadays.

Sandwich

Sandwich is such an everyday word that it is hard to remember that it came into common usage as a result of the fourth Earl of Sandwich's (1718–92) habit of calling for a slice of beef between two slices of bread so he would not have to leave the gambling table to eat a meal. In fact, the bread and meat/cheese/other filling snack had been in existence for some time before it was christened the sand-wich.

Saxophone

Antoine Joseph (or Adolphe, as he came to be known) Sax was a Belgian who came from a musical family. With his father, Charles Joseph, he produced a sax-horn, an instrument similar to a cornet; the sax-tuba, a large sax-horn which resembled the tuba; and, in 1846, the **saxophone**.

Shrapnel

In the late eighteenth century, General Henry Shrapnel invented a shell which exploded before reaching its target, releasing a shower of deadly missiles. It was called 'spherical case shot' by the British Army in 1803; but in June 1852, at the request of the General's family, the name was changed to 'shrapnel shell' – by which it was already widely known in any case. The word **shrapnel** has since come to mean metal splinters from other kinds of exploding shells.

Sideburns

The whiskers that some men wear down the sides of their cheeks were originally called 'burnsides' after Ambrose Everett Burnside, a popular hero of the American Civil War who wore them. No one is quite sure how the name became turned around to become **sideburns**!

Silhouette

Most of us know that **silhouette** means a drawing or cutout in which only the outline of the object portrayed is seen, the rest being filled in in black. They were popular in the eighteenth and nineteenth centuries, and were an inexpensive way of creating a portrait. This last fact is believed to be the reason why they were named after an unpopular and penny-pinching eighteenth-century French Minister of Finance called Etienne de Silhouette.

Stetson

This high-crowned, wide-brimmed cowboy hat which keeps off the sun and rain was originally made by John B. Stetson in Philadelphia in 1865. They became very popular and Stetson sold more than two million a year.

Tarmac

John Loudon Macadam was a Scotsman who was made Surveyor-general of roads in the Bristol area in 1815. He had long wanted to improve the rough roads of England, and devised a surface made of a layer of roughly broken stones covered by a layer of fine stones, which wore well and became known as **macadam**. But when cars first appeared on the roads in the early 1900s, it was decided to add a tar coating in order to bind together the top layer of stones; this surface became known as **tarmacadam** or simply **tarmac**.

Teddy bear

In November 1902 the President of the United States, Theodore Roosevelt, spared the life of a small brown bear while on a hunting expedition. The incident became the

subject of newspaper cartoons, and an enterprising New York shopkeeper produced a model of the bear in brown plush and displayed it in the shop window, next to one of the cartoons, with the label 'Teddy's bear'. The **teddy bear** soon caught on and became a great success, the manufacturer even writing to Mr Roosevelt asking his permission to call the bear after him. The President agreed and the rest is history.

Wellingtons

Wellingtons were originally fashionable leather boots which came up above the knee in front and were made popular by Arthur Wellesley, first Duke of Wellington, who defeated Napoleon at Waterloo – a far cry from the **wellies** we wear to galumph around in the mud or snow!

Zeppelin

A **zeppelin** is a large, rigid airship, the framework of which contains compartments filled with gas; it was named after its inventor, Count Ferdinand von Zeppelin, who was born in 1838. People travelled in a separate compartment slung below the main body of the ship; in the 1920s the *Graf Zeppelin* flew over a million miles and carried over 13,000 people. In 1937 a giant zeppelin called the *Hindenburg* caught fire, killing thirty-six people and signalling the end of the zeppelin era.

K Kindle of Kittens

Kindle is another word for 'litter', that is, a collective noun for a group of kittens. You will be familiar with the word **flock** to describe a group of sheep or birds, and the word **herd** to describe a group of cows. These words are also collective nouns — words which describe a group of things or animals.

There are dozens of collective nouns in existence, but how many can you think of? Here is a challenge that will remind you of a few of them. Match the collective nouns in the first column with the creatures in the second.

pride	cattle
covey	fish
host	geese
drove	lions
gaggle	partridges
school	sparrows

(Answers on page 157.)

Here are forty-two more collective nouns, some familiar, some quite unusual; all, I think, rather poetic and appealing.

a **colony** of ants
a **shrewdness** of apes
a **cete** of badgers
a **sloth** of bears
an **army** of caterpillars

a **parliament** of owls
a **congregation** of plovers
a **string** of ponies
a **nest** of rabbits
an **unkindness** of ravens

a **clowder** of rats
a **peep** of chickens
a **murder** of crows
a **dule** of doves
a **balding** of ducks
a **skulk** of foxes
a **husk** of hares

a **crash** of rhinoceroses
a **building** of rooks
a **pod** of seals
a **dray** of squirrels
a **murmuration** of
   starlings
a **mustering** of storks

a **cast** of hawks
a **brood** of hens
a **siege** of herons
a **harras** of horses
a **smack** of jellyfish
a **deceit** of lapwings
an **exaltation** of larks
a **leap** of leopards
a **plague** of locusts
a **watch** of nightingales

a **flight** of swallows
a **knot** of toads
a **hover** of trout
a **rafter** of turkeys
a **pitying** of turtledoves
a **bale** of turtles
a **gam** of whales
a **route** of wolves
a **descent** of woodpeckers

L   Left and Right Means a Fight

At least, in Cockney rhyming slang it does. A Cockney is someone born within the sound of Bow bells (the bells in the church of St Mary-le-Bow), in what is now the East End of London, but in former days was the heart of the city.

The rhyming slang used by Cockneys seems to have originated among the London 'underworld' – the criminal section of the community – back in the 1860s. It may have been intended as a kind of code which, if overheard by the wrong people, could not be understood.

One of the difficulties in understanding it is that often there are a number of phrases with the same meaning. Another is that people who speak it usually only say the first (non-rhyming) part of the rhyme. For example, the best-known rhyming-slang phrase, **apples and pears**, meaning stairs, becomes **apples**. When you hear someone use it, you rack your brains for a word that rhymes with apples and that can possibly have the correct meaning – and give up.

Sometimes the slang phrase is so complicated that you wonder if it is all worth it. For example, if someone said they were going along to the **Arthur to sausage a goose's**, it would take a bit of working out to realize that what they meant was that they were going to the bank (**Arthur** Rank) to cash (**sausage** and mash) a cheque (**goose's** neck)!

Here are some examples of Cockney rhyming slang, with their meanings.

Adam and Eve	believe
ain't it a treat	street
all afloat	boat
'a'penny dip	ship
apples and pears	stairs
'appy 'alf hours/April showers	flowers
army and navy	gravy
babbling brook	crook *or* cook
bag of coke	bloke
bag of yeast	priest
baker's dozen	cousin
Becher's Brook/butcher's hook	book (butcher's hook also means look)
bees and honey	money

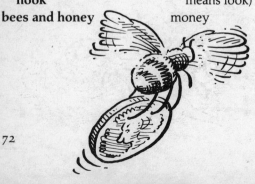

bottle and stopper	copper (police)
brass tacks	facts
brown bread	dead
cash-and-carried	married
cat and mouse	house
Charing Cross	horse ('cross' would be pronounced 'crorss')
cherry ripe	pipe
cloth and silk	milk
cocoa	know ('I should cocoa')
corns and bunions	onions
custard and jelly	TV (telly)
daisy roots	boots
Darby and Joan/ dog and bone	telephone
Davy Crockett	pocket
dicky dirt	shirt
dickory dock	clock
do as you like	bike
Dolly Varden	garden
Dover harbour	barber

earwig	twig (understand)
eighteen pence	sense
fisherman's daughter	water
fleas and itches	pictures (cinema) (pronounced 'pitchers')

France and Spain	rain
Gert and Daisy	lazy
ginger ale	jail
Glasgow Rangers	strangers
gypsy's warning	morning
hail and rain	train
half-inch	pinch (steal)
ham shank	Yank (American)
Harvey Nichols	pickles
has-beens	greens (vegetables)
heavens above	love
hit or miss	kiss

ice-cream freezer	geezer (a man)
I'll be there	chair
Irish stew	true
jacket and vest	West (West End of London)
Jeremiah	fire
Jim Skinner/Lilley and Skinner	dinner
Joe Brown	town
Joe Soap	dope (stupid person)
kidney punch	lunch
king's proctor	doctor
left and right	fight
lemon squash	wash
lion's lair	share
load of hay	day
lollipop	shop
Lucy Locket	pocket
Mary Lou	blue
me and you	menu (me 'n' you)
Mickey Mouse	house
Mother Hubbard	cupboard
mum and dad	mad
mutter and stutter	butter

75

mum & dad.

needle and thread	bread
Noah's ark	dark *or* nark (informer to police)
ocean pearl	girl
ocean wave	shave
old folks at home	comb
Oscar Claters (usually **Oscars**)	potatoes (taters)
overcoat maker	undertaker
'ow d'yer do	stew (a 'nice old 'ow d'yer do', i.e. a muddle, a 'goings-on')
peas in the pot	hot
pen and ink	stink
pig and roast	toast
pitch and toss	the boss
plates of meat (plates)	feet
pride and joy	boy
Queen's Park Rangers	strangers
rabbit and pork (rabbit)	talk
rats and mice	dice
Rawalpindi	windy
rock of ages	wages
Rosie Lee	tea
sausage roll	dole
shake and shiver	river

song of the thrush	brush
stand at ease	cheese
steak and kidney	Sidney
storm and strife/trouble and strife	wife
tar and feather	weather
this and that	flat (apartment)
tit for tat (titfer)	hat
Tommy Dodd	odd
tomfoolery	jewellery ('joollery')
two-foot rule	fool
two thirty	dirty
Uncle Ned	bed *or* head
upper deck	neck
Vicar of Bray	tray
whistle and flute	suit
whistle and toot	loot
Yarmouth bloater	motor (i.e. motor car)

From the *Word Box* Cockney dictionary, can you work out what the following passage says?

'There was a nice 'ow d'yer do on the hail and rain the other gypsy's warning. Two Queen's Park Rangers started a left and right – something about half-inching some tomfoolery. The first ice-cream freezer had seen this bag of coke in the Dolly Varden and reckoned he'd broken into the Mickey Mouse. I didn't know whether to Adam and Eve 'em or not. If you ask me, they were a pair of babbling brooks.'

(Answer on page 157.)

M   Madam, I'm Adam

At first sight, the title of this chapter may seem a little odd. At second sight it may seem even more so, for if you look carefully at it you will see that it reads the same either forwards or backwards. A word or phrase or even a sentence that does this is called a palindrome. The title of this chapter could be said to be the first palindrome ever – assuming they spoke English in the Garden of Eden!

The longest known palindromic word in the world is the nineteen-letter Finnish word *saippuakivikauppias*, which means 'a dealer in caustic soda'. American-Indian dictionaries contain a twelve-letter word, *kinnikkinnik*, which means 'a kind of tobacco made of dried leaves and bark'. The longest palindromic words in English are **redivider**, meaning 'something that divides again', and **rotavator**, originally a trade name for a mechanical digger but now accepted as an ordinary word.

Lots of shorter everyday words are palindromes: **nun**, **pip**, **pop**, **pup**, **boob**, **deed**, **noon**, **civic**, **kayak** and **level** are just ten of them. How many more can you think of?

And when you've finished thinking of palindromic words, try to devise some palindromic sentences. It isn't easy, but it can be done:

Was it a car or a cat I saw?
In a regal age ran I.
Yawn a more Roman way.
A man, a plan, a canal – Panama.

Was it Eliot's toilet I saw?
Ten animals I slam in a net.

The Emperor Napoleon was supposed to have said,
'Able was I ere I saw Elba,' and the writer Penelope Gilliatt
produced this amazing fifty-one-letter palindrome: 'Doc,
note I dissent. A fast never prevents a fatness. I diet on
cod.'

The trouble with most long palindromes is that they
don't make much sense, and therefore don't really count.
Try writing some short ones of your own. As you can
see, words like **was** and **saw** at the beginning and end are
very useful.

Easier to make up, and almost as much fun, are the kind
of palindromes that cheat slightly because, although the
sentences as a whole can be read backwards or forwards,

79

the words themselves are read forwards only. For example:

> God knows man. What is doubtful is what man knows
>   God.
> Bores are people that say that people are bores.
> So patient a doctor to doctor a patient so.
> Women understand men; few men understand women.
> Does milk machinery milk does?

Here you will notice that what makes the palindrome
work is using a word either as a verb or a noun (**doctor**)
or as an adjective or a noun (**patient**), or using a word
that looks the same but is quite different in meaning from
another word (**does**).

Now, what do you make of this?

> Dies slowly fading day, winds mournfully sigh,
> Brightly stars are waking;
> Flies owlet hooting, holding revel high,
> Nightly silence breaking.

It is a poem that tells the same story if you read it again
backwards, but word by word, not letter by letter. Try it
and see. And what about this?

> As I was passing near the jail
> I met a man, but hurried by.
> His face was ghastly, grimly pale.
> He had a gun. I wondered why?

Try reading it line by line, with the fourth line first,
followed by the third, second and then the first. You will
discover that it too can be read backwards, but this time
line by line rather than word by word.

Finally, let me introduce you to an old friend of mine, the semordnilap. You don't know what a semordnilap is? I bet you do! Here are a few:

bard, deliver, devil, dog, golf, mood, moor, rail, stop, strap, straw, stressed, yard.

Each word can be read backwards to make an entirely different word. Try reading semordnilap backwards, and what do you get? Palindromes, of course. There are lots of semordnilaps in our language. Try seeing how many you can list in five minutes.

N Nine Thumps Is Punishment

You may think that the chapter titles in this book get curiouser and curiouser, as Alice might have said, but 'nine thumps' really *is* 'punishment'. In the same way, 'conversation' is 'voices rant on'. Can you see why? It is because they contain the same letters rearranged in a different order. A word that is made up in this way is called an anagram, and is much loved by crossword compilers.

An anagram can be any kind of rearrangement of the letters, as long as they make a proper word or phrase, like 'rats' and 'star' or 'Monday' and 'dynamo'. To me, the most interesting are the anagrams which wittily highlight a meaning related to the original word. For example, an anagram of 'waitress' is 'A stew, sir?'; one of 'steamer' is 'sea term'; one of 'twinges' is 'we sting'.

Anagrams can also be made of phrases:

the eyes . . . they see
a shoplifter . . . has to pilfer
a decimal point . . . a dot in place?

Or they can be made out of famous people's names. Again, to make them amusing, they should be relevant to the person. Here is one of the name William Shakespeare: 'I ask me, has will a peer?' And here is one of Florence Nightingale: 'flit on, cheering angel!'

See if you can make anagrams out of the following words and phrases. The answers are given on page 158 – but don't give up too soon.

arid	persist
cheating	right
each	sauce
enraged	save
fringe	scale
ideas	sheet
indeed	study
meteor	tough
neigh	use
newt	weird

a cute call
a man's rag
chart ice circlet
court posers
Dan ties it on
got as a clue
heat's thrones
life's aim

made sure
seen as mist

Another amusing way of forming anagrams is to make them with exactly the opposite meaning to the words from which they are taken. In this case they are called antigrams. For example, an antigram of 'funeral' is 'real fun', one of 'misfortune' is 'it's more fun', and one of 'Santa' is 'Satan'. Here are some more:

arch saints/anarchists
enormity/more tiny
ill-fed/filled
infection/fine tonic
nice love/violence
restful/fluster

See if you can invent some apt antigrams of your own.

O Odd English

This chapter could be subtitled 'A Slice of Pidgin Pie' because it is about a form of English, originally used between Chinese people and Europeans trading in the Far East, which is called 'pidgin English'. The word **pidgin** is not a wrong spelling of the bird's name, but a Chinese corruption of the word 'business'. The language was arranged according to the Chinese idiom (or manner of speaking), and this is why it seems odd to us although, on the whole, we can understand it. For example, in pidgin the Duke of Edinburgh is called **fella-belong-Queen**, which makes sense, even if it seems a bit odd. The expression **chop chop!**, meaning 'quickly' or 'immediately', is an example of Chinese pidgin, as is the expression **long time no see**. They are such common expressions that we think of them as being English but, once you really look at them, their origin becomes apparent.

Chinese pidgin isn't the only kind that exists. A word that was originally pidgin English in the Western Pacific but has now come to be a generally accepted term is **'walkabout'**. Another which is heard reasonably often is **toe-ragger**. It is used to mean a contemptible person, and it comes from the Maori words *tua rika rika*, which mean 'a slave'.

The Creoles of the West Indies — people who were originally descended from Europeans or from African Negroes — have their own version of pidgin. If they want to describe something as 'big', they say **big fella**. From them we get the word **savvy**, to understand, and **piccaninny**, a small child. **Mary** means 'a woman', a sign of the Christian missionary influence, and the language itself is called **talky talky**. There are even road-signs in pidgin, such as **Ton Rait** for 'turn right'.

An example of pidgin English which some of you will recognize is shown below. You might know it well. Or do you?

> Papa belong me-fella, you stop long heaven
> All'e sancru 'im name belong you.
> Kingdom belong you 'e come.
> All 'e hear 'im talk belong you long ground
>   all same long heaven.
> Today givem kaikai belong day long me-fella.
> Forgive 'im wrong belong me-fella
>   all-same me-fella forgive 'im wrong all
>   'e makem long me-fella.
> You no bring 'em me-fella long try 'im.
> Take 'way some T'ing nogood for long me-fella.

Believe it or not, it is the Lord's Prayer.

P   Picture a Word

Clever people not only play games with words as words, they play games with words as pictures. Technically, a word picture is called a rebus, and it is defined as 'an enigmatic representation of a name, word or phrase by pictures, letters, numbers, or other words or phrases'. This is a complicated way of saying that if I write four letters like this:

M E

A L

I have what everyone should have every day, a square meal. Do you get it? Are you in the picture?

What's this?

OCE A N

Quite right, it's a drop in the ocean!

You will probably have come across this phrase before. Can you read it?

YYURYYUBICURYY4ME

You may find it easier if it is arranged like this:

YY U R YY U B I C U R YY 4 ME

The secret is not to try to read it as a word, but to read it (almost) letter by letter. Got it? (The answers to this and the next ten are on page 159.)

The word picture below is the title of a play by Shakespeare. Do you know what it is?

<pre>
        ADO
    ADO   ADO
    ADO   o   ADO
    ADO   ADO
        ADO
</pre>

Here is a phrase you will have heard many times. It means 'equal'. What is it?

ONE ANOTHER

ONE ANOTHER

ONE ANOTHER

ONE ANOTHER

ONE ANOTHER

ONE ANOTHER

If you are stuck, try it like this:

ONE	ANOTHER
ONE	ANOTHER
ONE	ANOTHER
ONE	ANOTHER
ONE	ANOTHER
ONE	ANOTHER

And here we have something that frequently happens in the British winter. It quite often happens in the British summer, too.

WETHER

This next one is really sneaky. It represents a phrase you might hear to describe a robbery in a cops and robbers film. What is it?.

JOANB

If you are stuck, try it like this.

JO an B

If you managed that one, try this. The picture represents a single word.

U^C_T

Here's another single word. It represents what might be left over from the Sunday joint.

B
E

They say that the Post Office is clever at deciphering strangely written addresses. Do you think they could make head or tail of this one?

Wood
Mary
And
Hants

And this one is something a lawyer might say to someone about to give evidence in court.

STAND   OATH
U   UR

To finish with, if you were in the habit of talking to teapots, you might say this to one after someone had drained the last dregs from it.

OICURMT

Finally, here's a toast to send you on your way.

S
M
O
T
T
O
B

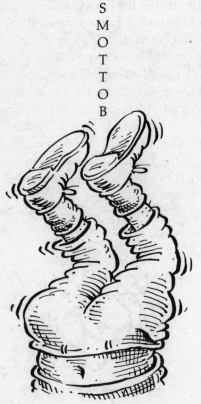

Q The Queen's English

You may retort, 'Of course she is! She's descended from William the Conqueror,' which would make her French, but never mind. In fact the apostrophe in this chapter's title does not imply the Queen 'is' anything; it indicates the possessive, that is, the English *belonging to* the Queen, which is another way of saying 'standard English'.

Standard English is the English which is generally accepted as correct. It does not include slang terms, or colloquialisms, or regional words, because if it did it might not be readily understood by the whole population.

Various regions of Britain (to say nothing of other parts of the world where English is spoken) have their own pronunciation and often their own words. If you visit those parts of the country that are far from where you live, you may notice that other people's speech can some-

times be almost incomprehensible. You may have to ask them several times to repeat what they said, and you can feel them thinking that you must be a 'foreigner', that is to say, someone from another part of the country.

This is partly because they may speak with a regional accent, laying the stress on a different part of a familiar word and thereby making it sound different, and partly because they may use words which are totally unfamiliar to you as a stranger, but which other people from the same area would understand.

Regional differences go back a long way. The original inhabitants of Britain were pushed into the far west and north of the country by waves of invaders from the east and south. These first Britons spoke the old Celtic tongue, which developed into Welsh, Cornish (now extinct but similar to Welsh), Manx and Gaelic. The south, east and Midlands of England were predominantly Anglo-Saxon, while northern and eastern England was influenced by Danish words. This has resulted in words like church in the south, and **kirk** in the north, because originally the *sh* and *ch* sounds were pronounced as *sk* and *k* in the north.

Other pronunciations have persisted into our own times. In the south-west of England an *f* is often pronounced as a *v*. So you might hear someone speak of a **varmer**, or of somebody's **vace**, meaning 'farmer' and 'face'. And words that begin with an *s* are pronounced as if they began with a *z*, so 'Somerset' sounds like 'Zummerzet'.

In the Greater London area people say **wye** for 'way', and speak with a curious gap in the middle of some words, known as a glottal stop, which leads them to say **bo'l** for 'bottle' and **bu'er** for 'butter'.

Pronunciation does not start or stop at a specific regional boundary, it changes gradually. For example, the Scots are noted for the way they roll their *r*s – a **burn** (Scots word for a stream) is pronounced 'burren' – and aspirate their *h*s in words like **where**, but these characteristics can be found in northern England too. In the far north, around the Newcastle area, where the dialect is known as Geordie, some of the words (for example, the use of **lass** or **lassie** to mean 'girl') are the same as those in Scotland.

Let's look at some specific areas and the way the people who live there speak and use different expressions.

The North-East

Here, as we have seen, there is a Scottish influence. People say **doon** for 'down', and **oot** for 'out', **bairn** for 'child' or 'baby', **gang** for 'go'. But some pronunciations sound as if they come from northern Ireland rather than Scotland, for example **hor** for 'her'. They will call you **pet** as a friendly name, whether they know you or not, or **hinny**, if they are being very friendly.

If, while you are there, you need to go to the lavatory, you ask for the **netty**. This is believed to come from an old euphemism for lavatory, 'necessary house'.

A number of words which are pronounced as one syllable in standard English, in Geordie are pronounced as two. 'Home' sounds like **hyem**, 'book' like **byuek**, 'bad' like **byadd**, 'there' like **theor**.

South Yorkshire

As in the northern part of the county, South Yorkshire uses **thee** and **thou** for 'you', pronounced **thi** and **tha**. So, for example, 'do it yourself' becomes **do it thi sen**. Following the success a few years ago of the film *Kes* (which many people in the south did not understand as the characters spoke in South Yorkshire dialect), a national newspaper published a glossary of typical terms. One of the most interesting was **If tha doan't gi' o'er as'll gi' thi a claart**, which of course means 'If you don't stop it I shall clout you.' It could equally be expressed as **A'll fetch thi one** − 'fetch' here meaning 'to give'.

If people in South Yorkshire talk of **a mort of** or **a power of** they mean 'a lot of'. If they talk of it **siling down**, they mean it is pouring with rain. If, after being in the rain, they say they are **perished**, they mean they are very cold; and if they constantly complain of the cold, they are described as **nesh**. Someone who complains and is a bit of a cry-baby is described as **mardy**. If people **flit**, they move house; if they **mither** (pronounced myther) they pester. If they are in pain, they complain of **gip**, and if the pain goes on and on, they say it **nages**. A boss is called a **gaffer**, sweets are called **spice**, a door-catch is a **sneck**, and the narrow passage between two houses a **gennel**. If they go to buy something, they may ask the vendor, **'What's the damage?'** meaning 'How much do I owe you? A hole is an **oil**, a baby a **babby**, and they don't wash but **wesh**. An ear is a **lug oil** and a mouth a **gob**, though these words are not used in polite company.

The Bristol area

Many people in Bristol call their city **Bristle**, which illustrates in essence how they speak. They tend to miss out a lot of letters and even whole syllables, and run words together. For example, 'after all' becomes **aft trawl**,

'bottom' becomes **bomb**, 'definitely' becomes **deaf knit**, 'minutes' becomes **mince** and 'months' becomes **munce**. If they went into a café, they might order **pine chips**, which sounds very peculiar until you realize it is pie and chips. They say **avenue** for 'haven't you', and if you were to ask someone the **krek** (correct) time, you might receive the answer **squaw pass sen**, meaning 'it's a quarter past seven'.

Cornwall

Cornwall, as we have seen, once had its own language which was similar to Welsh, though it died out in the last quarter of the eighteenth century. To me there is always a

feeling of being somewhere quite separate from the rest of England when you are in Cornwall. There are still Cornish people who have never been as far from home as Plymouth, which is **up country**, along with the rest of England.

If you are a tourist in Cornwall you may hear yourself described as an **emmett**. This is the local word for an ant, and the Cornish call tourists emmetts because of their slow progress, with their endless cars and caravans clogging narrow country lanes. A Cornishman is known as **Cousin Jack**, and he is supposed to have dealings with the **piskies** or little people, rather like the Irish with their leprechauns. If he is feeling well disposed towards you, he will call you **m'love**, **m'lover**, or even **mi 'andsome**. People say, 'By Tre, Pol and Pen you can tell the Cornishmen' and these three syllables are often the prefixes to Cornish people's names and place-names. **Tre** means house, **Pol** means a fortress, and **Pen** means a headland. If something is done well in Cornwall, they make **a proper job** of it.

Scotland

Scotland still has its own language, and if you go there you may hear it spoken in country districts. When they are speaking English, the Scots have a very distinctive accent; the odd thing is, the further into the country you get and the further away from cities and large centres, the less pronounced the accent becomes. So while you may find a heavy Glaswegian accent almost impossible to understand, if you travel out to the Highlands and the Western Isles you will find the accent very soft and gentle and hardly noticeable.

As we have seen, the Scots roll their *r*s, and speak in a more precise and clipped manner than do the English. They say **aye** for 'yes' and **noo** for 'no', and tend to drop the final letter off words like yourself, so it becomes **your-**

sel'. You may have heard the expression **Dinna fash yoursel'**, meaning 'don't put yourself out'. They say **gang** for 'go', **wee** for 'little', **muckle** for 'large'. A boy is a **laddie** and a girl a **lassie**. A child is a **bairn** or a **wean** — **wee ane** — and if it is well grown or pretty, it is **bonny**. If you pick it up and whirl it round, you are **birling**. A bread-roll is a **bannock**, a horse is a **cuddy**, and a cold, wet, raw winter day is described as **dreich**. (This -*ch* ending is difficult for the English to pronounce, for it is softer than the *k* sound the English often make, for example when they say 'lock' for **loch**, but not as soft as the *sh* sound.) A **brae** is a hill and **ben** means 'mountain', a **glen** is a valley, and a **firth** is an estuary and is related to the Norse word **fjord**.

R Right, Rite, Write!

A brake may break, a band may be banned, deer may be dear and a fillet may fill it. And, I suppose, a horse may be hoarse and a hare certainly has hair. By now you must have guessed that this chapter is about words that sound exactly the same but are spelt differently and have different meanings. In other words, it is about homophones.

There are lots of homophones in the English language, and they often lend themselves to jokes. For example:

SMITH: What would you do if you got up in the morning, hadn't got any clothes on, and met a ferocious bear?

JONES: *Run!*

SMITH: What, with a bear (bare) behind!

Some homophones have three words, for example:
need, kneed, knead;
pear, pair, pare;
furs, firs, furze.
There are at least six homophones connected with parts
of the body. Can you list them all? (Answers on page
ooo.)

Now see if you can pick the correct word from each
pair listed below to insert in the gaps in the following
paragraph.

Sidney, the - - - -'s son, was having a - - - - in the sun.
It was - - - -, and he'd just finished his - - - -, a - - - - of
- - - - - - - -. Outside the - - - - grazed in the paddock.
The - - - - was a bit - - - -, but she had a lovely long
- - - -. A - - - - made him look up – the - - - - in the - - - -
shoes had come in to complain that the cat had - - - -
his mother's - - - -. 'Oh - - - -,' said Sidney, 'I expect
he'll - - - - to be - - - - from the bedroom. He is a bad
- - - -!'

pear.   pair of pears.   pair of pared pears.

band/banned
bark/barque
boll/bowl
boy/buoy
cereal/serial
Claude/clawed
coarse/course
dear/deer
firs/furs/furze
graze/greys

knead/need/kneed
lays/laze
made/maid
maize/maze
morning/mourning
mare/mayor
shake/sheikh
sloe/slow
suede/swayed
tail/tale

(Answers on page 159.)

S S.O.S.

There can hardly be a reader who doesn't know that
S.O.S. is the international distress signal. It is transmitted
in Morse code, the best known of all codes, by three dots,
three dashes and three dots, and is therefore instantly
recognizable, even by people whose knowledge of Morse
is imperfect. Some people think S.O.S. stands for 'Save
Our Souls', but it doesn't. The letters were chosen in 1910
simply because they could be transmitted by wireless
quickly and clearly, not because they had any special
meaning.

In our lives of late twentieth-century rush and bustle
we are surrounded by abbreviations. Some have been
standard for many years and appear in dictionaries, such
as **e.g.**, which is short for the Latin *exempli gratia*, meaning
'for example'. Some consist only of the words' initial
letters, given in capital letters, like **BBC** for British
Broadcasting Corporation. Some have lower-case letters
as well, such as **St**, standing for both street and saint, **Dr**
for doctor, when it is a form of address, **Col.** for colonel,
and so on.

In addition, in the modern world we have abbreviations
which are called acronyms — abbreviations pronounced as
if they were words rather than as a series of letters. Some
of these are so well known that you probably think they
are words in their own right. Take, for example, the word
laser. It isn't really a word at all, but an acronym. To be
strictly correct, we should write it out like this: L.A.S.E.R.,

as the letters stand for 'light amplification by stimulated emission of radiation'. A more obvious acronym is **NATO**, which stands for the North Atlantic Treaty Organization; and another is **Oxfam**, which is really the Oxford Committee for Famine Relief. And have you heard of a **quango**? It is really a quasi non-governmental organization!

Here are six acronyms. Do you know what they stand for?

ASLEF
ILEA

NALGO
RADA
radar
Unesco

(Answers on page 160.)

And do you know what the following abbreviations stand for, and whether they are acronyms or not? (In the book publishing world, it is usual to put a full stop after the shortened forms of a word only when the abbreviation does not include the word's final letter, as in Jan. for January, etc. for *et cetera* (from the Latin meaning 'and so on'), etc.)

adj.	HQ	OED
B.Sc.	IBA	O
Bt	IoW	quasar
Co.	km/h	qt
COD	LTA	SALT
Fr.	MBE	SAS
FRCVS	MD	Sgd
GMT	Messrs	UFO
HB	NB	VHF
HMSO	NEDC	wpb

(Answers on page 160.)

T The Quick Brown Fox Jumps Over a Lazy Dog

Pangrams

The title of this chapter is a pangram. Why? Because it contains every letter in the alphabet. Pangrams are fun to devise, and not too difficult if you don't mind how long they are. **The quick brown fox jumps over a lazy dog** contains thirty-three letters; it is well known to typists, as they often use it to test their machines. Thinking of typewriters made me produce this next one. It cheats a bit because it uses a name, but it shows how easy it can be to construct a pangram: **Typewriter daze makes John fight back, quelling vexation.** (Forty-eight letters)

The Book of Ezra, in the Bible, contains a pangram with the exception of the letter *j* (an odd letter, sometimes a variant of *i*, and not used at all in some languages, for example, Italian). Here it is:

> And I, even I Artaxerxes the king, do make a decree to all the treasurers which are beyond the river, that whatsoever Ezra the priest, the scribe of the law of the God of heaven, shall require of you, it be done speedily.

That's a pangram containing a mere 172 letters!

Pangrams with rather fewer letters include:

Pack my box with five dozen liquor jugs. (Thirty-two letters)

The five boxing wizards jump quickly. (Thirty-one letters)

It is very difficult to compose a pangram consisting of fewer than thirty-one letters without using names. Here's one with twenty-nine letters:

Quick wafting zephyrs vex bold Jim.

And here's one with twenty-eight:

Waltz, nymph, for quick jigs vex Bud.

(A good pangram word, 'vex'.) And, for good measure, here's one with twenty-six:

J. D. Schwartz flung Q. V. Pike my box.

To make a twenty-six-letter pangram without names, you have to use archaic words. The following, in everyday

English, means 'carved figures on the bank of a fjord in a rounded valley which irritated an eccentric person'. Here it is:

Cwm, fjord-bank glyphs vext quiz.

Apart from that, the only other non-name twenty-six-letter pangram I have come across is this amazing sentence which appears in the *Guinness Book of Records*:

Veldt jynx grimps waqf zho buck.

Apparently it means, 'A wryneck woodpecker from the African grasslands climbs up the side of a male ox grazing on sacred Muslim-owned land.' So there.

Alphabetics

If devising twenty-six-letter pangrams is a bit beyond you, have a go at alphabetics. This is much easier; it involves constructing sentences in which each word begins with a successive letter of the alphabet. Hyphenated words can count as one word or two, which makes it even easier. Here is an American example:

> A brilliant Chinese doctor exhorted four graduating hospital interns: 'Just keep looking, men – no other prescription quickly relieves sore throats, unless veterinarians wilfully X-ray your zebras.'

And here is an advertisement from *The Times* newspaper in 1842, which proves that our ancestors did have a sense of humour:

> **TO WIDOWERS AND SINGLE GENTLEMEN – WANTED** by a lady, a SITUATION to superintend the household and preside at table. She is Agreeable, Becoming, Careful, Desirable, English, Facetious, Generous, Honest, Industrious, Keen, Lively, Merry, Natty, Obedient, Philosophic, Quiet, Regular, Sociable, Tasteful, Useful, Vivacious, Womanish, Xantippish, Youthful, Zealous, &c.

(Xantippish means 'like Xantippe, the wife of Socrates'.) Again, note the absence of the *j*.

The triumph of alphabetics must surely be this epic poem, called 'The Siege of Belgrade'. The author is unknown, and it, too, has no *j*.

An Austrian army, awfully arrayed,
Boldly by battery, besieged Belgrade;
Cossack commanders cannonading come –
Dealing destruction's devastating doom;
Every endeavour, engineers essay,
For fame, for fortune – fighting furious fray: –
Generals 'gainst generals grapple – gracious
    God!
How honours Heaven, heroic hardihood!
Infuriate – indiscriminate in ill,
Kindred kill kinsmen, – kinsmen kindred kill!
Labour low levels loftiest longest lines –
Men march 'mid mounds, 'mid moles, 'mid
    murderous mines:
Now noisy, noxious, noticed nought
Of outward obstacles opposing ought:
Poor patriots, partly purchased, partly pressed:
Quite quaking, quickly quarter, quarter quest,
Reason returns, religious right redounds.
Suvorov stops such sanguinary sounds.
Truce to thee, Turkey – triumph to thy train!
Unjust, unwise, unmerciful Ukraine!
Vanish vain victory, vanish victory vain!
Why wish we warfare? Wherefore welcome
    were
Xerxes, Ximenes, Xanthus, Xaviere?
Yield! ye youths! ye yeomen, yield your yell!
Zeno's, Zapater's, Zoroaster's zeal,
And all attracting – arms against acts appeal.

Next time you have an hour or two (or three or four) to
spare, try writing an alphabetic poem of your own.

U   U. F. Biggles, Ph.D.

Let me introduce you to **U. F. Biggles, Ph.D.** He's not a distant cousin of the fictional First World War air ace Biggles (more correctly known as Captain James Bigglesworth, D.S.O., D.F.C., M.C.), he's not even a real person. He's a mnemonic.

What's a mnemonic? It's a device to aid the memory and it gets its name from Mnemosyne, the Greek goddess of memory. A mnemonic usually consists of a memorable phrase, the initial letters of which can be used as a key to something you need to remember but find difficult. Dr Biggles was created by a friend of mine, Robert McLardy, who uses the mnemonic to remember the names of the twelve countries that make up the European Economic Community. U. F. Biggles, Ph.D., stands for United Kingdom, France, Belgium, Italy, Germany, Greece, Luxembourg, Eire, Spain, Portugal, Holland and Denmark.

Your teachers have probably taught you other mnemonics. If you study music, you will know that the notes on the lines of the stave, reading upwards, are E, G, B, D, F, which can be remembered by Every Good Boy Deserves Favour. And the biologists among you may know that you can recall the names of the excretory organs of the body by remembering not a phrase but a single word: **SKILL**. SKILL gives you the Skin, Kidneys, Intestines, Liver, Lungs.

The struggle to remember the order in which battles occurred can be helped with good mnemonics. This one applies to the Wars of the Roses: **A Boy Now Will Mention All The Hot, Horrid Battles Till Bosworth.** As I probably don't need to tell you, this stands for: St Albans, Blore Heath, Northampton, Wakefield, Mortimer's Cross, St Albans II, Towton, Hedgeley Moor, Hexham, Barnet, Tewkesbury and Bosworth. **Richard Of York Gave Battle In Vain** was the first mnemonic I learnt. Oddly enough, it has nothing to do with the Wars of the Roses. It is designed to help you remember the colours of the rainbow: red, orange, yellow, green, blue, indigo, violet.

Once you get into specialist areas of study, mnemonics become both more complicated and more necessary. If you were studying the anatomy of the frog, you could remember the order in which its arteries branch off the aorta, the main artery from the heart, by **Little Men In Short Black Mackintoshes**, which is a lot easier to remember than lingular, mandibular, innominate, subclavian, brachial and musculocutaneous.

I once made up a mnemonic to help me remember the order of the Great Lakes in America, from north and west to south and east: **Saddle Many Horses, Elephants and Ostriches**; in other words, Superior, Michigan, Huron, Erie and Ontario. While on the subject of riding, a friend who's rather keen on it tells me that the letters marking the points round a small dressage arena, A, K, E, H, C, M, B and F, can be remembered by **All King Edward's Horses Carry Many Boring Fools**.

Why not make up some mnemonics of your own? The one essential is that they should be easy for *you* to remember because, if they aren't, you might as well try and remember the thing they were supposed to be helping you to remember instead!

V A Vixen Is a Female Fox

A vixen is a female fox, but an oxen is not a female ox. In fact, you can't say 'an oxen', because oxen is the plural form of ox. If fox A meets fox B we have two foxes, but if ox A meets ox B we have two oxen. The **-en** ending is in fact a very old form of plural, and survives in words like **women** and **children**.

Before we go on to plurals, let us consider masculine and feminine forms of words. It is fashionable nowadays to pretend there is no difference between the two, and to try to find a word that is neither male nor female to replace anything that hints of masculinity or femininity.

So, instead of 'chairman', we have **chairperson**, despite the fact that to many people a 'chairman' could denote someone of either sex. But when it comes to animals we really have to accept the difference between the sexes. A bull is a very different proposition from a cow, after all! (Interestingly, the word **fox** can mean an animal of either sex; if you want to speak of a male fox, you should say a **dog fox**.)

If you had been brought up in France, the matter of gender for nouns would not present you with any problems. You would know that words like *table* and *fenêtre* ('table' and 'window') are feminine, and words like *pain* and *chien* ('bread' and 'dog') are masculine.

Look at the list of words below. Some of the words denote the masculine, some the feminine, and some can mean either. See if you can spot which is which, and give the opposite gender where it exists.

author	drake	nurse
baron	earl	peacock
bitch	goose	pen
blonde	heifer	pig
boar	ladybird	queen
cock	lion	ram
colt	lord	shepherd
count	mare	tiger
deacon	marquis	viscount

(Answers on page 161.)

The oddities of English plurals are summed up nicely in this very clever poem sent to me by Mrs Dorothy Rawle of Birstall in West Yorkshire. The poem is called 'The English Language'.

We'll begin with *box;* the plural is *boxes,*
But the plural of *ox* should be *oxen,* not *oxes.*
One bird is a *goose,* but two are called *geese,*
Yet the plural of *moose* should never be *meese.*
You may find a lone *mouse,* or a whole nest of
      mice,
But the plural of *house* is *houses,* not *hice.*

If the plural of *man* is always called *men,*
Why shouldn't the plural of *pan* be called *pen?*
The *cow* in the plural form may be *cows* or *kine,*
Yet a *bow,* if repeated, should never be *bine,*
And the plural of *vow* is *vows* and not *vine.*

117

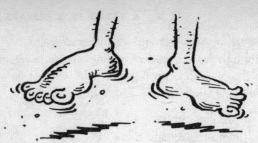

If I speak of a *foot* and you show me two *feet*,
And I give you a *boot*, would a pair be called
   beet?
If one is a *tooth* and a whole set is *teeth*,
Why shouldn't the plural of *booth* be called *beeth*?

If the singular's *this* and the plural is *these*
Should the plural of *kiss* be written as *keese*?
Then one may be *that*, and two would be *those*,
Yet *hat* in the plural should never be *hose*,
And we speak of a *cat*, but we don't say two *cose*!

We speak of a *brother* and also of *brethren*,
Yet though we say *mother*, we never say *methren*!
Then the masculine pronouns are *he*, *his* and *him*,
But imagine the feminine — *she*, *shis* and *shim*!

So English, I'm sure you all will agree,
Is the funniest language there ever could be.

Apart from the curious forms pointed out in the poem,
there are other things to catch us out regarding the adding
of an *s* or *es* to make singular words plural. *Es* is an older
form of a plural ending, and is generally applied to words
that end in vowels, such as **domino** — but the rule does
not always apply! What are the plurals of the following
words?

camera	**dingo**
cargo	**domino**
cinema	**opera**
dado	**sombrero**

Words ending in vowels are not the only ones that may
either take *s* or *es* in the plural. What about the three
words below? How do you form their plurals?

bus   crocus   focus

(Answers on page 162.)

Some words change their last letters completely in the
plural. For example, what is the plural of **data**? Does that

question strike you as odd? It should do, because **data** is already the plural of **datum**. A similar pair are **stratum** and **strata**. But what about **medium**? If we are talking about a means of communication, **by medium of**, then the plural is **media** – a popular collective term nowadays for the press, radio and television. But if we are talking about the kind of person who claims to be able to put us in touch with the dead, then the plural is **mediums**.

There are words like **fish**, and certain kinds of fish, which stay the same whether singular or plural. For example, you may have one **goldfish** or two **goldfish**, the

word is the same. For supper the family may have **trout**, not trouts, or, for a special occasion, **salmon**, not salmons. But even here, words are not consistent, for if we have more than one sardine we speak of **sardines**.

Certain other creatures are similar to 'fish' in their plural form. For example, **deer**, **sheep**, and game birds such as **grouse** and **partridge** are the same in the singular as in the plural. What about **cows**? You may have one cow and two cows, but a herd may consist of either **cows** or **cattle**. (Or, if you read Dorothy Rawle's poem, **kine**, but that word is old-fashioned nowadays.)

Hyphenated words, and other words that are not

hyphenated but are composed of two or more separate words, can also cause problems. What do you suppose are the plurals of these three?

daddy-long-legs   **mother-in-law**   **teaspoonful**

Words of more than one syllable that end in *y* usually change the *y* to an *i* and add *es* to form their plurals, for example: **dairy** − **dairies**; **duty** − **duties**. Can you think of any that don't?

For those who found all the plurals so far very easy, here are some real challenges. See if you know, or can work out, or can guess, the plurals of these.

cherub	**madame**
crisis	**plateau**
gateau	**sarcophagus**
index	**seraph**
lieutenant-colonel	

(By the way, a cherub is a little winged angel with a human face, a seraph is a six-winged angel, and a sarcophagus is a stone coffin!)

(Answers on page 162.)

GATEAU

W   Walter's a Wally

I'm not being rude, Walter really is a Wally. For **Wally** is a shortened, pet form of the name Walter, as are Walt and Wat. Forget the modern, not very polite meaning of the word 'Wally', and you may be surprised to learn that **Walter** means 'ruling people' and comes from an Old German source. It was made popular by the Normans from the eleventh century onwards.

All names have a meaning, whether they be first names, surnames or the names of places, rivers and mountains. Let's list some first names first, together with their origins and meanings.

Adam   Hebrew; 'redness'
Alan   Welsh and Breton; believed to mean 'rock' and 'noble'
Andrew   Greek; 'manly'
Ann(e)   Hebrew, from **Hannah**; 'grace', 'favour'
Ant(h)ony   Latin, from **Antonius**; meaning unknown

Barbara   Latin, from Greek; 'strange', 'foreign'
Beatrix/Beatrice   Latin; 'happy'
Bernard   Old German; 'bear', 'brave'
Brian   unknown origin, believed to be Irish; 'hill'
Bridget   Irish; 'the high one', 'strength'

Carol(ine)   Italian feminine form of **Charles**, Old English for 'man' or 'husband'
Catherine   Greek; meaning uncertain, possibly 'pure'

Cheryl   derived from **Cherry**, a form of **Charity**, a seventeenth-century Puritan 'virtue' name

Christopher   Greek; 'one who carries Christ in his heart'

Clive   from surname, meaning 'cliff'

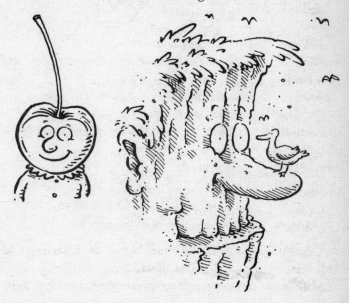

Darren from an Irish surname used as a Christian name

David Hebrew; 'God is my judge'

Derek modern form of **Theodoric**, Old German; 'ruler of the peoples'

Diana Latin; from word meaning 'divine'. Diana was the goddess of hunting and the moon

Douglas Gaelic; 'dark water'

Edward Old English; 'property guardian'

Eileen Irish, probably a form of the Greek **Helen**; 'bright/shining one'

Elizabeth Hebrew; 'oath of God/God's perfection'

Emma Old German; 'all-embracing'

Ernest German; 'vigour'

Felix Latin; 'happy'

Florence Latin; 'flourishing'

Frances/Francis Latin; 'a Frenchman'

Frederick Old German; 'peaceful ruler'

Gail variant of **Abigail**, Hebrew; 'my father rejoices'

Gemma Italian; 'precious stone'

Geoffrey   Old German; 'peace'

George   Greek; 'earth-worker, husbandman, farmer'

Giles   a French form of a Latin word derived from the Greek meaning 'young goat'

Gillian   English form of the Latin **Juliana**, which probably meant 'descended from Jove'

Hayley   English place-name and surname meaning 'hay meadow'

Heidi   German form of **Adelaide**; 'nobility'

Henry   Old German; 'home ruler'

Hilary   Latin; 'cheerful'

Hugh   Old German; 'mind, soul, thought'

Ian   Scottish form of **John**

Ingrid   Old Norse; 'beautiful'

Irene   Greek; 'peace'

Isabel/Isobel   Spanish and Portuguese forms of **Elizabeth**

Ivan   Russian form of **John**

Jacqueline   French feminine form of **Jacques** (**James**)

James   Latin; 'a supplanter'

Jane   Latin; feminine form of **John**

Jennifer   Welsh; 'fair, white', a variant of **Guinevere**

John   Hebrew; 'Jehovah has been gracious'

Judith   Hebrew; 'Jewish'

Karen   Danish form of **Katarina**, see **Catherine**

Kelly   Irish surname meaning 'strife' or 'warlike', used as Christian name

Kenneth   Gaelic; from two words meaning 'fair one' and 'fire-sprung'

Kevin   Irish; 'handsome at birth'

Kit   early pet-name for **Christopher**

Laura   Latin; 'bay (tree) or laurel'

Leonard   Old German; 'strong as a lion'

Leslie/Lesley   from a Scottish place-name, meaning unknown, that became a surname

Lester   phonetic form of place-name **Leicester**

Linda   German; from a word meaning 'serpent', a symbol of wisdom

Lionel   Latin; 'little lion'

Lisa   form of **Elizabeth**

Lucy   English form of Roman **Lucia**, meaning 'light'

Margaret   Greek; 'pearl'

Mary   the Greek form of the Hebrew **Miriam**, meaning of which is uncertain

Matthew   Hebrew; 'gift of the Lord'

Maurice   Latin; 'Moorish, dark-skinned'

Michael   Greek form of a Hebrew name; 'who is like the Lord'

Nadia   Russian; 'hope'

Neil   Irish; 'champion'

Nicholas   Greek; 'victory people'

Nigel   Latin; a variation of **Neil**

Nina   Russian; a pet form of names like **Annina**, **Antonina**

Oliver   possibly Old German, meaning 'elf-host'

Oscar   Old English; 'god-spear'

Oswald   Old English; 'god-power'

Pamela   apparently invented by Sir Philip Sidney in 1590

Patricia   Latin; 'noble'
Paul   Latin; 'small'
Peter   Greek; 'stone, rock'
Philip/Philippa   Greek; 'lover of horses'

Queenie   adapted from the word 'queen'
Quentin   Latin; a saint's name

Ralph   Old Norse; from words meaning 'counsel' and 'wolf'
Richard   Old German; 'strong ruler'

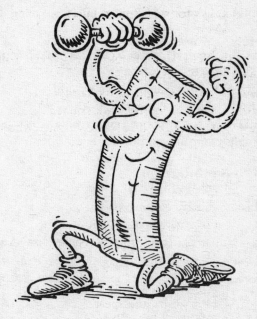

Riley   Irish surname used as a first name, meaning 'valiant'
Robert   Old English; 'fame-bright'

Roger   Old English, Old German; from words meaning 'fame' and 'spear'

Rosemary   Latin; originally from a word meaning 'dew of the sea' and not from the herb

Sally   a pet form of **Sarah**

Samantha   from **Samuel**, Hebrew; 'name of God'

Sarah   Hebrew; 'princess'

Sean   Irish form of **John**

Sharon   Hebrew; 'the plain'

Sophia/Sophie   Greek; 'wisdom'

Stephen   Greek; 'crown'

Susan   Hebrew; 'lily'

Tabitha   Aramaic; 'gazelle'

Thomas   Hebrew; 'twin'

Tiffany   Greek; 'manifestation of God'

Timothy   Greek; 'honouring God'

Tracey/Tracy   a Norman place-name which became an English surname and then a first name

Trevor   Welsh; 'great homestead' or 'sea homestead'

Una   an old Irish name of uncertain meaning

Ursula   Latin; 'bear'

Valerie   Latin; 'to be strong'

Vanessa   invented by Jonathan Swift (1667–1745)

Veronica   Latin; 'true image'. A woman named Veronica was said to have wiped the face of Christ at Calvary with a cloth which then bore the impression of his face

Victor   Latin; 'conqueror'

Victoria   Latin; 'victory'

Vincent   Latin; 'to conquer'

Wayne   from the USA; 'a maker of wagons'
William   Old German; 'will-helmet'
Winifred   Welsh; 'blessed reconciliation'
Winston   from the surname, which is derived from a
place-name meaning 'wine's settlement'

Xanthe   Greek; meaning 'yellow, fair or golden'

Yolande   modern French form of **Iolanthe**, from the
Greek words for 'violet' and 'flower'
Yvonne   French; from the German for 'yew wood'

Zachary/Zachariah   Hebrew; 'Jehovah has re-
membered'
Zara   Arabic; 'splendour or brightness of the east'
Zoë   Greek; 'life'

In early times nobody had a surname; but gradually, as
people began to make clear the difference between, for
example, John who lived on the hill and John who was a
blacksmith, they would add a word on to the end of the
first name. It was a bit like the Welsh, with all their
Joneses, referring to 'Jones the milk', 'Jones the post', and
so on.

These added-on names, which grew into the surnames
we know today, came into being in the fourteenth century.
They referred either to a person's trade or occupation
(for example a **fletcher**, someone who makes arrows
= **Fletcher**); to the place where they lived (for example
on the hill = **Hill**); or to their appearance (for example a
dark-haired person would be called **Brown** or **Black**).
Some names, of course, could be misleading. A person
given the surname **Long** or **Longfellow** may indeed have
been very tall, or he may have been just the opposite!

Sometimes people were named after animals and birds. A man who was considered cunning might be called **Fox**, one who was strong, **Bull**, one who was wild and fierce, **Wolf**. **Spink** comes from the sound a chaffinch makes, and was the name given to a cheerful person, while a noisy, quarrelsome individual was called **Sparrow**.

Here are the origins and meanings of some of our commoner surnames:

Adams named after the biblical character
Andrews named after the saint
Aziz 'dear'

Baker after the trade
Barber after the trade
Brown 'dark-haired' or 'dark-skinned'

Champion the largest and toughest knight
Cohen a priest
Cox from the male bird, cock, meaning a lively and rather aggressive young man, much the same as our word 'cocky' means today

Davies/Davis after St David

Dixon   Dick's (Richard's) son
Dolittle   'lazy'

Edwards   after the first name
Evans   after the Welsh first name **Evan**

Faulkner   a falconer
Ford   the first Fords lived by a ford
Frost   a nickname for someone pale and/or white-haired

Good   a shortened form of the Anglo-Saxon **Godwin**, 'good friend', or **Godric**, 'good ruler'
Green   from the May Day ritual of garlanding a man with greenery – the Green Man
Grey   from the hair colour

Hancock   derived from the first name **John**
Hughes   from the first name **Hugh**
Hussein   'excellence'

Ibbotson   from the girl's name **Isabel**

Jennings   from the name **John**
Jolly   from the characteristic, originally from the French word *joli*
Jones   from **John**

Kennedy   Irish; meaning 'ugly head'
King   from the May Day celebrations – the King of the May

Lamb   a nickname for a blond, curly-haired lad
Lawrence   from St Laurence
Li   'a plum tree'
Longbottom   'a narrow, deep valley'

Mason   a stone-worker
Merryweather   'a good-tempered man'
Morris   'dark like a Moor, Moorish'

Newman   a stranger
Nichols   after St Nicholas
Norman   from Normandy

O'Connor   **O** means 'son of', **Conor** was an early
Irish king

Paine   pagan, a heathen
Patel   village headman
Pearce   after St Peter
Powell   from **ap-Howell**, the son of **Howell**, who
was a Welsh prince

Reid   'red-haired'
Richardson   the son of **Richard**
Roper   a rope-maker

Sharp(e)   'a fierce and brave fighter'
Singh   'lion'
Smith   a blacksmith
Spencer   someone in charge of the food in a medieval household, the 'dispenser'

Taylor   a tailor
Thwaite   a clearing in the forest
Trueman   as it sounds

Vaughan   'small'
Vincent   after the saint

Wainwright   a wagon-maker
Webster   a weaver
Wood   a woodcutter

Young   as it sounds, originally a nickname

Many surnames, such as **Ford** and **Thwaite** in the list above, come from places. And the place-names of Britain derive from many languages: Celtic, Anglo-Saxon, Norse, French and Latin.

The earliest names are the Celtic ones, coined by the earliest inhabitants of the British Isles. **Avon**, now the name of several rivers, simply meant 'river' originally. An early word for 'water', which the Romans wrote as *isca*, developed into the rivers **Exe** and **Axe**. The word from which the rivers **Thames**, **Tamar**, **Tame** and **Teme** were named meant 'dark'.

Many place-names end in **ton**, which was originally an

133

old word meaning 'enclosure, encampment or farm'. It is from this word that our word 'town' has developed. The prefixes of **ton** describe the town or settlement. **Norton** was in the north, **Sutton** in the south, **Weston** in the west, and **Aston** or **Easton** in the east. **Kingston** meant that the place was connected with the king; **Shepton** or **Shipton** related to sheep; **Leighton** to vegetables and, in particular, leeks.

In northern and eastern England, the Danes influenced the naming of places and settlements. Their equivalent for the word **ton** was **by** or **thorp**, so their farms and settlements were called **Ashby**, the farm with the ash trees; **Selby**, the farm with the sallows (a kind of willow); **Scunthorpe**, the farm of a man who squinted. They called a church a **kirk**, and many northern place-names – **Kirkby Stephen**, **Kirkby Lonsdale** – contain this word.

The Saxons called a farm a **wick**, from which we get names like **Chiswick**, a cheese farm; **Gatwick**, a goat farm; and **Woolwich**, which produced wool. A landing place was a **hithe**, from which names like **Rotherhithe** have developed; and a river was crossed at a **ford**, bridges being few and far between in those days. This has led to lots of place-names, such as **Oxford**, where oxen crossed; **Stratford**, where a Roman road crossed a river, **Stamford** or **Stanford**, a stony ford.

French names, such as **Beaulieu** (*beau lieu*, beautiful place) come from the Normans, though sometimes the spelling has been changed, as in **Bewdley** in Worcestershire. Another French name is **Richmond**, 'rich hill', which was given to the Yorkshire town four hundred years before the Surrey one, which was named after an Earl of Richmond. French influence can also be seen in compound place-names, such as **Chapel-en-le-Frith**. **Chapel** and **en le** are French words – meaning chapel and 'in the', but **frith** is an old English word, meaning 'wood'. So the name means 'the chapel in the wood'.

From the Romans came the **chester**, **cester** and **caster** endings. These words meant a camp, which developed into a town, and these settlements were frequently on rivers. The existing river-name was retained, and the Roman suffix added to it, to give place-names like **Doncaster**, on the River Don, **Exeter**, on the Exe, **Towcester**, on the Tove, and the town of **Chester** itself.

Latin names were sometimes added on to existing ones by the monks who kept public records, as they were almost the only people who could write. They would add words like **magna** and **parva** to village names, to denote the larger and smaller hamlets, or **episcopi**, meaning 'of the bishops', such as in **Kingsbury Episcopi**. But the name **regis**, 'king', was added to **Bognor** on the south coast only in the early part of the twentieth century after George V had stayed there.

X X Words

X words are, of course, crosswords, the most popular form of puzzle that exists.

Crosswords

Crosswords originated in America. The very first was a diamond-shaped puzzle with no black squares, and it was published in a newspaper called the *New York Sunday World* on 21 December 1913. It was compiled by an Englishman named Arthur Wynne, who called it a Word-Cross. It was immediately popular with the newspaper's readers and so, the following week, it was followed by another. By mid-January the name had been changed to Cross-Word. The crossword was born, and from that time has never looked back. Here is the world's first crossword puzzle.*

* Reproduced with permission from *What's Gnu? A History of the Crossword Puzzle* by Michelle Arnot, published by Vintage Books (Random House), New York, 1981.

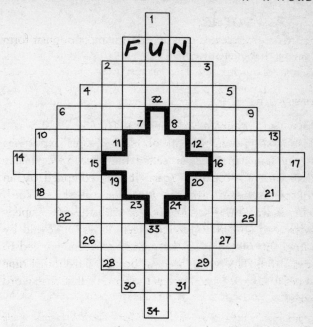

2–3	What bargain hunters enjoy.
4–5	A written acknowledgment.
6–7	Such and nothing more.
10–11	A bird.
14–15	Opposed to less.
18–19	What this puzzle is.
22–23	An animal of prey.
26–27	The close of a day.
28–29	To elude.
30–31	The plural of is.
8–9	To cultivate.
12–13	A bar of wood or iron.
16–17	What artists learn to do.
20–21	Fastened.
24–25	Found on the seashore.
10–18	The fibre of the gomuti palm.

6–22	What we all should be.
4–26	A day dream.
2–11	A talon.
19–28	A pigeon.
F–7	Part of your head.
23–30	A river in Russia.
1–32	To govern.
33–34	An aromatic plant.
N–8	A fist.
24–31	To agree with.
3–12	Part of a ship.
20–29	One.
5–27	Exchanging.
9–25	Sunk in mud.
13–21	A boy.

(Solution on page 163.)

Riddles

It seems that ever since man has had language he has been fascinated by puzzles. The earliest example of this fascination is believed to be the riddle. In Greek mythology the Sphinx posed the question: 'What walks on four legs in the morning, on two legs at midday, and on three legs in the evening?' It was Oedipus who eventually provided the correct answer, 'Man', because he walks on all fours when he is a baby (the morning of his life), on two legs when he is grown (midday) and with the aid of a stick (three legs) when he is old (the evening of his life). The Greek poet Homer was said to be so upset by a riddle put to him by some fishermen – 'What we caught we threw away: what we could not catch we kept' – that it hastened his death. Can you guess the answer? It's really very simple if you consider what life must have been like in those days, that is to say the eighth century BC. The answer is 'fleas'!

Word squares

The earliest forerunner of the crossword is probably the word square. In about the third century AD, an Egyptian called Moschion carved a grid consisting of 1,521 Greek letters in alabaster. From its central starting point a message could be read up, down, backwards or forwards, in the same way as words can be traced in a modern word-track puzzle. Even earlier in date was a much simpler twenty-five-letter word square, which was discovered in the mid-nineteenth century in the Roman excavations at Cirencester, and again in the 1930s in Pompeii, just south

of Naples, when the city was excavated. It is a kind of acrostic, and it looks like this:

 R O T A S
O P E R A
T E N E T
A R E P O
S A T O R

It can be read from left to right, right to left, upwards and downwards, and means both 'Arepo the sower holds the wheels with force' and 'The sower Arepo holds the wheels at work'.

Word puzzles have been popular down the centuries, but they really came into their own a hundred and more years ago during the reign of Queen Victoria. All sorts of word puzzles were printed in Victorian periodicals and in special little puzzle books, and the Queen herself was said to have composed a number of puzzles, her favourites being acrostics.

Acrostics

An acrostic is a puzzle in which clues that read across give individual answers that read across, but in which can be read another word or words that read down. For example, a very short acrostic might read like this:

1. Worn on the upper half of the body   **S**hirt
2. Worn by a Scotsman   **K**ilt
3. Special boots are worn for this   **I**ceskating
4. Worn in wet weather   **R**aincoat
5. Worn after a bath?   **T**owel

All the answers are things to wear, as is the hidden word which reads down the initial letters, **SKIRT**.

More about crosswords

If nineteenth-century Britons were enthusiastic about acrostics, twentieth-century Americans were wild about crosswords. Following the popularity of Arthur Wynne's early efforts in 1913 and 1914, readers began to contribute puzzles of their own to the paper. A kind of crossword fever hit the United States. It was reported that Americans were devoting five million hours a day – mostly during their working hours – to solving crossword puzzles, and this was seen by some people as a social evil.

Library staff were instructed to black out crosswords in newspapers to prevent people from keeping them too long. One Los Angeles library chained its dictionaries to a desk at standing height and allowed people to spend only five minutes at a time using them. In a Chicago court, a judge sentenced a husband to no more than three crosswords daily, as his wife had claimed he was neglecting his business. Even the fashion industry became involved, with dresses featuring crossword prints, and jewellery composed of tiny crosswords in gold and silver settings.

It was 1924 before a crossword first appeared in a British newspaper, and that was an American puzzle syndicated to the *Sunday Express*. The British had rather pooh-poohed the crossword mania of the USA, and a lot of people said it would never take off in Britain. They were wrong. The crossword very quickly overtook the acrostic in popularity. It was said to be particularly welcomed by pickpockets, who would sneak up on unsuspecting puzzlers in hotel lobbies and similar places, while they were deeply engrossed in their crosswords, and snatch their wallets!

The early crosswords had straightforward clues. For example, Arthur Wynne's puzzles included clues like 'an animal of prey' and 'found on the seashore', for which the answers were **lion** and **sand**. Then along came the cryptic clue. Cryptic means 'hidden, secret, mysteriously obscure' – and that's what the new clues were meant to be.

A literary critic and translator called Edward Powys Mather had found crosswords intriguing, but thought their simple clues rather dull. So he compiled some puzzles of his own, using puns and anagrams, to make the clues cryptic. Here is an example: 'A Scot counts his own ingredients', the answer to which is **cost**. It is an anagram of 'Scot' ('Scot's ingredients'), is something one counts, and is also a bit of a joke, since the Scots are reputed to be very careful with their money.

Mather became crossword correspondent of the *Observer*, and his puzzles appeared under the pseudonym of Torquemada, who was a fifteenth-century Spanish inquisitor. Mather developed the crossword still further. In the very early days, crosswords appeared in all kinds of shapes, but then it was decided to standardize their construction. They should be symmetrical, interlocking, and one-sixth of the squares at most should be black. But Torquemada also devised a new kind of crossword, which did away with the black squares altogether, instead separating words with heavy black lines and so filling the entire grid with letters.

Nowadays practically all of the world's daily newspapers include a crossword puzzle. But one of the most well known, that in *The Times*, did not appear until February 1930. The newspaper had resisted the crossword as a short-lived, new-fangled idea, but finally had to bow to public pressure. The first puzzle for *The Times* was constructed by someone who had never set one before, a young man named Adrian Bell. It was the start of a long career: Bell also compiled *The Times*'s Golden Jubilee crossword, which appeared in 1980.

Crosswords are obviously here to stay. If you find most cryptic ones too difficult, try the simpler, 'quick' ones which appear in most newspapers. To be good at solving crosswords you need a good general knowledge, and to be able to spell. Access to reference books helps, too: a dictionary, an atlas and the works of Shakespeare are all valuable. You can even buy special books like rhyming dictionaries, and lists of two-, three-, four-, five-, six-, seven-, eight-letter words and anagrams — though I feel that to go to those lengths is rather defeating the object of solving a puzzle.

If you are quite good at crosswords and fancy trying to set one, keep it simple to start with. A professional setter uses a symmetrical grid, and between a half and three-quarters of the letters are used in more than one word. About half the letters in each word should also appear in another word so as to give the solver a little help. A conventional size is fifteen squares by fifteen squares, about a sixth of which are black. If you are trying to set

cryptic clues, try breaking the word down into its syllables. For example, if you wanted to set a cryptic clue for the word 'banana', you can think of it as 'ban', 'an' and 'a'. So your clue might be 'A fruit forbids two indefinite articles' — **banana** being the fruit, **ban** being 'forbids', and **an** and **a** being the two indefinite articles. Fit the words into the grid *before* working out the clues or you will discover that you are wasting your time with words that cannot be fitted in.

Happy puzzling!

Y Yankee Doodle's Dandy

The writer Oscar Wilde once jokingly said, 'The English have really everything in common with the Americans, except, of course, language.' Between American English and British English there are certainly a lot of differences. We spell some words differently for a start. The British **cheque** is **check** in the US, **colour** is **color** and **traveller**, **traveler**. We also have different vocabularies. Take a look at this paragraph. If you understand every single word, then your American English is pretty good.

> Monday was a legal holiday and a school recess, so the Smith family went to the seaside. They ate cotton candy, had a ride on a roller coaster, and went to a restaurant for lunch. While they were waiting for the check, Jimmy Smith was surprised to see a large man in knickers walk past. Mrs Smith went to wash up, and then they went for a ride in the automobile, with its trunk crammed with seashells. They stopped for popsicles at the side of the road, and Jimmy had potato chips as well.

How did you get on? If you didn't do very well, you will find the answer on page 163. The fact of the matter is that Americans do use quite separate words from the British for certain things, and sometimes a British English word can mean something quite different to an American. For example, imagine yourself walking into a building four storeys (floors) high. Suppose you wanted to visit someone who lived on the floor at the top of the first flight of stairs. You would say you were going to the **first floor**. But if you were an American, you would say you were going to the **second floor**, because Americans count what the British call the ground floor as the first floor. It's all very confusing!

To help lessen the confusion, here is a short dictionary of British English/American English. If you couldn't understand the paragraph above before, you should be able to when you have studied this.

American English	*British English*
airplane	aeroplane
apartment	flat
automobile	car
bobby pin	hair grip
booth	kiosk (telephone)
can	tin
candy	sweets
check	bill (restaurant)

146

closet	wardrobe
comforter	eiderdown
cookie	biscuit (sweet)
cotton candy	candy floss
cracker	biscuit (not sweet)
crib	cot
cuffs	turn-ups (trouser)
diaper	nappy (baby's)
divided highway	dual carriageway
do the dishes	wash your hands
drugstore	chemist's shop
elevator	lift
faucet	tap
freeway	motorway
French fries	chips
gas(oline)	petrol
grade crossing	level crossing (railway)

hood	bonnet (of car)
intermission	interval
jelly roll	Swiss roll (cake)
jump rope	skipping rope
kerosene	paraffin
knickers	plus fours (golfing trousers)

legal holiday	bank holiday
love seat	settee
mail box	pillar box
mortician	undertaker
orchestra seats	stalls (theatre)
paddle	bat (for ball games)

parka	anorak
pit	stone (fruit)
pitcher	jug
popsicle	iced lolly
potato chips	crisps
pot holder	oven cloth
precinct	district

148

public school	state school
recess	break (school)
roller coaster	big dipper
round-trip ticket	return ticket
sack lunch	packed lunch
sales clerk	shop assistant

scratch pad	scribbling pad
sheers	net curtains
shorts	pants (underwear)
slingshot	catapult
sneakers	plimsolls
stand in line	to queue
stove	cooker
stroller	pushchair (child)

suspenders	braces
sweater	jumper
tag	label
traffic circle	roundabout (road)
trailer truck	articulated lorry
truck	lorry
trunk	boot (of car)
undershirt	vest
vacation	holiday
vest	waistcoast
wash cloth	face flannel
wash up	wash your hands
wharf *or* pier	quay
yard	garden
zero	nought
zip code	postal code
zucchini	courgettes

Z   Zoo Talk

The other morning, feeling dog-tired, I was walking
  sluggishly to school,
When I happened upon two girls I know – who were
  busy playing the fool.
They were monkeying about, having a fight –
But all that they said didn't sound quite right.
'You're batty, you are – and you're catty too.'
'That's better than being ratty, you peevish shrew!'
'Don't be so waspish!' 'Don't be such a pig!'
'Look who's getting cocky – your head's too big!'
'You silly goose! Let me have my say!'
'Why should I, you elephantine popinjay!'
I stopped, I looked, I listened – and I had to laugh
Because I realized then, of course, it's never the cow or
  calf
That behave in this bovine way.
It's mulish humans like those girls I met the other day.
You may think I'm dogged, but something fishy's going
  on –
The way we beastly people speak of animals is definitely
  wrong.
Crabs are rarely crabby and mice are never mousy
(And I believe all lice deny that they are lousy).
You know, if I wasn't so sheepish and if I had my way
I'd report the English language to the RSPCA.

I wrote that poem because I thought how unfair it was that the language belonging to a nation of animal-lovers should contain so many words and phrases that are downright rude about animals. I don't think bats are batty and I know cats aren't catty, so it's not really right that when we want to call someone crazy or unkind we say they're batty or catty. It's not right, but we do it all the same.

Animals feature in lots of English expressions and usually in a rather unflattering way. Here are fifteen more words and phrases that relate to human behaviour but involve the names of animals. Do you know what they mean? And do you think they are fair to the animals or not?

to badger   a bird-brain
a bear with a sore head   a busy bee

153

chicken
eagle-eyed
to fox
to get one's goat
to hog
to horse around

to hound
to lionize
a toad/toady
a turkey
a worm

(Answers on page 164.)

I'm sure you're no bird-brained worm. I expect you're an eagle-eyed busy bee. If you are, why don't you try to invent some *new* expressions that use animal words to describe human behaviour in a friendly rather than a nasty way? Good luck.

Answers

B Blindworms Aren't Blind

1. **biannual** – twice a year, half-yearly
2. **biennial** – every two years
3. **canasta** – a card game
4. **canister** – a metal box
5. **comforter** – a scarf
6. **comforter** – something or someone who comforts
7. **dinghy** – a small boat
8. **dingy** – dirty, drab
9. **noisome** – foul-smelling
10. **noisy** – making a noise

C Coffee Pots and Donkeys

CARGO – ship's freight

E Eggs Mark the Spot

1. Because it's no use until it's been cracked.
2. When it's parquet (parky).
3. Because they come in packs.
4. Because one word leads to another.

5. Because it didn't give a hoot.
6. It gets hopping mad.
7. When he has a sty(e) in his eye.
8. Because it was import-ant.
9. A vicious circle.
10. March fourth.

H Hangman

EYE	FLOUR	TEA	MINE	DOG
AYE	FLOUT	TEN	MINT	DOT
APE	FLOAT	TIN	MIST	COT
APT	GLOAT	TIT	MOST	CAT
OPT	GROAT	TOT	MOOT	
OAT	GREAT	HOT	FOOT	
PAT	TREAT		FOOL	
PET	TREAD		COOL	
LET	BREAD		COAL	
LEE				
LIE				
LID				

I I Before E Except After C

CORRECT SPELLINGS ARE:
necessary, spaghetti, piccolo, coolly, definitely, disappointment, exuberant, malicious, manageable,

parallel, threshold, vocabulary, woolly.

INCORRECT SPELLINGS ARE:
accomodation should be **accommodation**;
ecstacy should be **ecstasy**;
excusible should be **excusable**;
flourescence should be **fluorescence**;
harrassment should be **harassment**;
investegate should be **investigate**;
occurence should be **occurrence**;
permissable should be **permissible**;
posession should be **possession**;
rythm should be **rhythm**;
seperate should be **separate.**

K   Kindle of Kittens

a *pride* of lions
a *covey* of partridges
a *host* of sparrows
a *drove* of cattle
a *gaggle* of geese
a *school* of fish

L   Left and Right Means a Fight

'There was a nice *goings-on* on the *train* the other *morning*.
Two *strangers* started a *fight* – something about *pinching*

some *jewellery*. The first *geezer* had seen this *bloke* in the *garden* and reckoned he'd broken into the *house*. I didn't know whether to *believe* them or not. If you ask me, they were a pair of *crooks*.'

N   Nine Thumps is Punishment

arid . . . raid

cheating . . . teaching

each . . . ache

enraged . . . angered

fringe . . . finger

ideas . . . aside

indeed . . . denied

meteor . . . remote

neigh . . . hinge

newt . . . went

persist . . . stripes

right . . . girth

sauce . . . cause

save . . . vase

scale . . . laces

sheet . . . these

study . . . dusty

tough . . . ought

use . . . sue

weird . . . wider

a cute call . . . calculate

a man's rag . . . anagrams

chart ice circlet . . . the Arctic Circle

court posers . . . prosecutors

Dan ties it on . . . destination

got as a clue . . . catalogues

heat's thrones . . . hearthstones

life's aim . . . families

made sure . . . measured

seen as mist . . . steaminess

P   Picture a Word

Too wise you are, too wise you be, I see you are too wise for me (2Ys U R, 2Ys U B, I C U R 2Ys 4 ME)

Much Ado About Nothing

Six of one and half a dozen of another

A bad spell of weather

An inside job. (**an** inside **JOB**)

Continue. (**C** on **T** in **U**)

Bone. (**B** on **E**)

Mary Underwood, Andover, Hants (Hampshire). (**Mary** under **Wood**, **And** over **Hants**)

You understand you are under oath (**U** under **Stand**, **U R** under **Oath**)

Oh, I see you are empty!

Bottoms up!

R   Right, Rite, Write!

feat/feet, hair/hare, heal/heel, knows/nose, sole/soul, toe/tow.

The words should be inserted in the paragraph in the following order:
sheikh, laze, morning, cereal, bowl, coarse, maize, greys, mare, slow, tail, bark, maid, suede, clawed, furs, dear, need, banned, boy.

S S.O.S.

The acronyms are:

ASLEF (Associated Society of Locomotive Engineers and Firemen);

ILEA (Inner London Education Authority);

NALGO (National and Local Government Officers' Association);

RADA (Royal Academy of Dramatic Art);

radar (**ra**dio **d**etection **a**nd **r**anging);

UNESCO (United Nations Educational, Scientific and Cultural Organization).

All these abbreviations are pronounced as if they were words.

The abbreviations stand for the following (acronyms are marked with an asterisk):

adj. – adjective;

B.Sc. – Bachelor of Science;

Bt – baronet;

Co. – company or county;

COD – cash on delivery;

Fr. – French;

FRCVS – Fellow of the Royal College of Veterinary Surgeons;

GMT – Greenwich Mean Time;

HB – hard and black (pencils);

HMSO – Her Majesty's Stationery Office;

HQ – headquarters;

IBA – Independent Broadcasting Authority;

IoW – Isle of Wight;

km/h – kilometres per hour;

LTA – Lawn Tennis Association;

MBE – Member of the Order of the British Empire;

MD – doctor of medicine;

Messrs – *messieurs* (French for 'gentlemen');

NB – *nota bene* (Latin for 'note well');

***NEDC** – National Economic Development Council ('Neddy');

OED – Oxford English Dictionary;

O – oxygen (chemical symbol);

* **quasar** – quasi-stellar object (an astronomical term);

qt – quiet ('on the qt');

* **SALT** – Strategic Arms Limitation Talks;

SAS – Special Air Services;

Sgd – signed;

UFO – unidentified flying object;

VHF – very high frequency;

wpb – wastepaper basket.

V   A Vixen is a Female Fox

author – can be either, authoress is now old-fashioned;

baron is masculine, feminine is **baroness**;

bitch is feminine, masculine is **dog**;

blonde is feminine, masculine is **blond**;

boar is masculine, feminine is **sow**;

cock is masculine, feminine is **hen**;

colt is masculine, feminine is **filly**;

count is masculine, feminine is **countess**;

deacon is masculine, feminine is **deaconess**;

drake is masculine, feminine is **duck**;

earl is masculine, feminine is **countess**;

goose is feminine, masculine is **gander**, though generally speaking 'goose' could be used to mean either;

heifer is feminine, masculine is **bull-calf** or **steer**;

ladybird can be either;

lion is masculine, feminine is **lioness**;

lord is masculine, feminine is **lady**;

mare is feminine, masculine is **stallion**;

marquis is masculine, feminine is **marchioness**;

nurse can be either, but men nurses are often called **male nurses**, and a male 'staff nurse' is a **charge nurse**;

peacock is masculine, feminine is **peahen**;

pen is feminine (it is a swan), masculine is **cob**;

pig can be either;

queen is feminine, masculine is **king** (people), **tom** (cats);

ram is masculine, feminine is **ewe**;

shepherd can be either but was generally masculine, with **shepherdess** as feminine;

tiger can be either, but is more usually masculine, with **tigress** feminine;

viscount is masculine, feminine is **viscountess**.

cameras, cargoes, cinemas, dados, dingoes, dominoes, operas, sombreros.

buses, crocuses, focuses.

daddy-long-legs, mothers-in-law; teaspoonsful (strictly speaking, but more usually **teaspoonfuls** nowadays).

The only one I can think of is **Hail Marys**, the Roman Catholic prayer addressed to the Virgin Mary.

cherubim or cherubs, crises, gateaux, indices, lieu-
tenant-colonels, mesdames, plateaux, sarcophagi,
seraphim.

X X Words

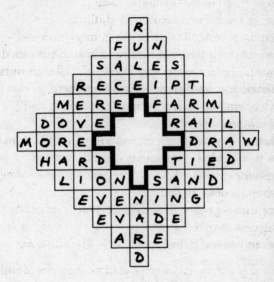

Y Yankee Doodle's Dandy

Monday was a **bank holiday** and a school **break**, so the
Smith family went to the seaside. They ate **candy floss**,
had a ride on a **big dipper**, and went to a restaurant for
lunch. While they were waiting for the **bill**, Jimmy Smith
was surprised to see a large man in **plus fours** walk past.

Mrs Smith went to **wash her hands**, and then they went for a **drive** in the **car**, with its **boot** crammed with sea-shells. They stopped for **iced lollies** at the side of the road, and Jimmy had **crisps** as well.

Z   Zoo Talk

to badger – to pester, torment or tease (as dogs do to badgers)

a bear with a sore head – a bad-tempered person

a bird-brain – a stupid person

a busy bee – an industrious person

chicken – a coward, or cowardly

eagle-eyed – having very good eyesight, being observant

to fox – to deceive or trick

to get one's goat – to irritate

to hog – to take the greater part of something for oneself

to horse around – to fool about

to hound – to pursue

to lionize – to treat as a celebrity

a toad/toady – a detestable or disgusting person/a hanger-on

a turkey – a failure, a flop (an American term applied to stage plays, etc.)

a worm – an insignificant or contemptible person

COME SING, JIMMY JO

Katherine Paterson

An absorbing story about eleven-year-old Jimmy Jo's rise to stardom, and the problem of coping with fame.

COME BACK SOON

Judy Gardiner

Val's family seem quite an odd bunch and their life is hectic but happy. But then Val's mother walks out on them and Val's carefree life is suddenly quite different. This is a moving but funny story.

AMY'S EYES

Richard Kennedy

When a doll changes into a man it means that anything might happen ... and in this magical story all kinds of strange and wonderful things do happen to Amy and her sailor doll, the Captain. Together they set off on a fantastic journey on a quest for treasure more valuable than mere gold.

ASTERCOTE

Penelope Lively

Astercote village was destroyed by plague in the fourteenth century and Mair and her brother Peter find themselves caught up in a strange adventure when an ancient superstition is resurrected.

THE HOUNDS OF THE MÓRRÍGAN

Pat O'Shea

When the Great Queen Mórrígan, evil creature from the world of Irish mythology, returns to destroy the world, Pidge and Brigit are the children chosen to thwart her. How they go about it makes a hilarious, moving story, full of totally original and unforgettable characters.

THE PRIME MINISTER'S BRAIN

Gillian Cross

The fiendish DEMON HEADMASTER plans to gain control of No. 10 Downing Street and lure the Prime Minister into his evil clutches.

JASON BODGER AND THE PRIORY GHOST

Gene Kemp

A ghost story, both funny and exciting, about Jason, the bane of every teacher's life, who is pursued by the ghost of a little nun from the twelfth century!

HALFWAY ACROSS THE GALAXY AND TURN LEFT

Robin Klein

A humorous account of what happens to a family banished from their planet Zygron, when they have to spend a period of exile on Earth.

SUPER GRAN TO THE RESCUE

Forrest Wilson

The punchpacking, baddiebiffing escapades of the world's No. 1 senior citizen superhero – Super Gran! Now a devastating series on ITV!

TOM TIDDLER'S GROUND

John Rowe Townsend

Vic and Brain are given an old rowing boat, which leads to the unravelling of a mystery and a happy reunion of two friends. An exciting adventure story.